What People Are Saying About

Living the 10 Commandments in New Times . . .

"After reading this book, I've changed my belief that living according to God's Commandments is something I can wait to do until I get older. As a teen with a hugely complicated life, I need God's hand upon me now. This book helped me see not only how important the Commandments are to my life, but how much I need God's blessings upon me."

Robbie Davis, 16

"Too many people worry about the Ten Commandments hanging on a wall, when the real issue is having them alive in our hearts. This book gives blood, pulse and soul to those rules to live by."

Terry Pluto
author and columnist, *Akron Beacon Journal*

"Just recently some students at my school got into a conversation about the Ten Commandments. One girl rolled her eyes and said, 'Oh, please, nobody believes in those anymore!' But two days later when I told her something, she asked, 'Is that really true? Do you swear on a stack of Bibles?' Well, correct me if I'm wrong, but I believe telling the truth falls under the ninth Commandment! It just goes to show you that when we're looking for *ultimate* truth, we're willing to call upon God and let His Commandments govern!"

Lannie Tarrenton, 15

"Bettie B. Youngs gives all of us, young and old, a lot to think about in her latest book. She makes the Ten Commandments come alive in a remarkable fashion and forces all of us to take a thorough inventory of our lives."

Pat Williams
Senior Vice President, Orlando Magic
author, *How to Be Like Jesus*

"Too many people lack the courage to talk about how incredibly important and central the Commandments are to daily living. The truth is, we rely upon them all the time, whether to give meaning to our lives or simply to keep some semblance of order in them. We must stop deluding ourselves into thinking that the Commandments are too outdated, too complicated or too far beyond our ability to apply them to our lives. This book will help you see the Commandments for all they are."

Derrick Charett, 21

"This book will help you understand the simple abundance in the Commandments—time-honored laws, perfectly formulated common sense, a plan for living a happy, productive and principle-centered life. I recommend this incredibly loving book as a gift to someone you love and care about because we do not 'break' the Ten Commandments . . . rather, we can become 'broken' if we do not follow their God-given wisdom."

Linda Fuller
cofounder, Habitat for Humanity International

"After my first boyfriend and I broke up, I discovered he had been chasing another girl while we were still together. Once he'd made her his new girl—without so much as letting me know our relationship was in trouble—he broke things off with me. I was hurt and felt so betrayed: What gave him the right to think it was okay for him to hold my hand, kiss me and tell me sweet things when he wasn't being genuine with me? Anyone who lives according to the Commandments knows we're to treat each other with kindness, dignity and respect. If I'd been dating someone who lived according to the principles spelled out in the Commandments, he'd have had the courage to talk things over with me, giving both of us a chance to end our relationship on good and true terms—even if his leaving broke my heart. Are the Commandments still relevant? Yes, they're just incredible common sense about how we're to love, respect and treat each other."

Kathryn Tilly, 17

"Regardless of where we stand on displaying the Ten Commandments—whether in school halls or courthouses—no one can stop us from displaying them in our homes or discussing them with our family and friends. If we want our young people to grow in faith, we need to talk about the Commandments and what they mean for our lives. This excellent and very thorough book can help families do that. Hanging the Ten Commandments on the wall may be symbolically important, but how a family lives them is much more crucial."

Nancy Rivard
founder, Airline Ambassadors

"Suddenly, why we need to 'follow the rules' makes a lot more sense. This very special book provides a valuable, timely and easily relatable set of guidelines for young adults today."

Stephanie Woodend
field director, Prison Fellowship Ministries

Living the 10 Commandments in NEW Times

A Book for Young Adults

Bettie B. Youngs, Ph.D., Ed.D.

Bestselling author of
the *Taste Berries™ for Teens* series,
*A Teen's Guide to Christian Living: Practical Answers
to Tough Questions About God and Faith*
and *12 Months of Faith: A Devotional
Journal for Teens*

Faith Communications
A Division of Health Communications, Inc.®

Health Communications, Inc.
Deerfield Beach, Florida

www.faithcombooks.com
www.tasteberriesforteens.com

All Scripture quotations, unless otherwise indicated, are taken from the Holy Bible, New International Version® (NIV®).

Library of Congress Cataloging-in-Publication Data is available from the Library of Congress.

Publisher: Faith Communications
        An Imprint of Health Communications, Inc.
        3201 S.W. 15th Street
        Deerfield Beach, Florida 33442-8190

Cover design by Andrea Perrine Brower
Inside design by Dawn Von Strolley Grove

To: _____

With Love and Blessings!

From: _____

Whoever has my commands and obeys them,
he is the one who loves Me.

John 14:21

Show me your ways, O Lord, teach me your paths;
guide me in your truth and teach me
for you are God my Savior, and my hope is in you all day long.

Ps. 25:4–5

Also by Bettie B. Youngs, Ph.D., Ed.D.

12 Months of Faith: A Devotional Journal for Teens (Faith Communications)

A Teen's Guide to Christian Living: Practical Answers to Tough Questions About God and Faith (Faith Communications)

365 Days of Taste-Berry Inspiration for Teens (Health Communications, Inc.)

A Teen's Guide to Living Drug-Free (Health Communications, Inc.)

A Taste-Berry Teen's Guide to Setting & Achieving Goals (Health Communications, Inc.)

Taste Berries for Teens #3: Inspirational Stories and Encouragement on Life, Love, Friends and the Face in the Mirror (Health Communications, Inc.)

A Taste-Berry Teen's Guide to Managing the Stress and Pressures of Life (Health Communications, Inc.)

More Taste Berries for Teens: A Second Collection of Inspirational Short Stories and Encouragement on Life, Love, Friendship and Tough Issues (Health Communications, Inc.)

Taste Berries for Teens Journal: My Thoughts on Life, Love and Making a Difference (Health Communications, Inc.)

Taste Berries for Teens: Inspirational Short Stories and Encouragement on Life, Love, Friendship and Tough Issues (Health Communications, Inc.)

Taste-Berry Tales: Stories to Lift the Spirit, Fill the Heart and Feed the Soul (Health Communications, Inc.)

A String of Pearls: Inspirational Stories Celebrating the Resiliency of the Human Spirit (Adams Media)

Gifts of the Heart: Stories That Celebrate Life's Defining Moments (Health Communications, Inc.)

Values from the Heartland: Stories of an American Farmgirl (Health Communications, Inc.)

Stress & Your Child: Helping Kids Cope with the Strains & Pressures of Life (Random House)

Helping Your Child Succeed in School (Active Parenting)

Safeguarding Your Teenager from the Dragons of Life: A Guide to the Adolescent Years (Health Communications, Inc.)

Keeping Our Children Safe: A Guide to Emotional, Physical, Intellectual and Spiritual Wellness (John Knox/Westminster Press)

Getting Back Together: Repairing the Love in Your Life (Adams Media)

Contents

Contents

Foreword

Some years ago, we stayed at a brand-new hotel in Israel. We were their very first guests! But the hotel was not really ready for customers in any way. Not only had the plastic not been removed from the pillows, but there were no railings on the balconies! To discourage guests from going out on the balcony in the first place—and thereby avoid the risk of getting hurt, perhaps even from falling off—a pole had been placed in the track of the sliding doors to block it shut. But with a view of the Mediterranean beckoning, we most definitely wanted a better look! It didn't take long for us to remove the pole, push the sliding glass doors wide open and walk out onto the balcony. Without the railings, however, the fear of falling was so terrifying that we quickly went back into the room. And so from our room on the fifteenth floor, we were never able to get a full view of the splendor of the beautiful Mediterranean, nor appreciate the fresh sea breezes the room provided. What a loss.

The next night we were in another high-rise hotel at the Sea of Galilee. This was a well-established hotel, most definitely ready to receive guests. Our room was on one of the top floors, and again we had a balcony overlooking the sea. This time, we opened the door to the balcony with confidence. We went bounding out and thoroughly enjoyed the view and fresh air. We leaned against the rail, looking all around and stayed out there for some time. We even left the door open for several hours so we could feel the cool breeze. It was glorious!

What was the difference between our two experiences? Boundaries. Unlike the first hotel, the solid boundary provided by the balcony of the second hotel allowed us the freedom to enjoy the view without feeling intimidated by the fear of falling or getting hurt in any way. That's the power of boundaries. A boundary—while it may sound limiting—actually provides freedom in that it shows where "safe" begins and ends. The Ten Commandments are boundaries—God's boundaries—to keep us safe.

Like the railings that surround a balcony, the Commandments, figuratively speaking, allow us to open the doors of our lives to the world and to "take a better look"—and to do so confidently, knowing where "safe" begins and ends. In a way, then, the Commandments are God's "railings" showing us how to live our lives with rambunctious zeal and "full-on" courage—yet without falling prey to destructive vices or unwise and unhealthy choices that separate us from God and from knowing His love. The Commandments, therefore, do not restrict us, but rather, protect and free us. We know where the barrier is that separates right from wrong, good from bad, and safe from unsafe. As a result, we are freed to live joyous lives filled with meaning, purpose and direction. This is why we are so enormously pleased that our friend and author Dr. Bettie Youngs has written a most important book on the subject of boundaries for living for young adults. As you'll discover in this most insightful and incredibly loving book, God wants, even expects, you to live a glorious and victorious life. In this book you'll discover how each of the Commandments are designed to help you do just that.

Living the 10 Commandments in New Times will make the Commandments come alive for you and help you see how important each one is to your day-by-day happiness. Moreover, you will see how loving and awesome God is, and how His Commandments were designed to help you become all that you were meant to be! As parents of four—with two teens still at home—we know this book will have a lasting positive impact on your life and for those with whom you share it.

Rev. Dr. Robert A. Schuller, Pastor
Donna M. Schuller, C.N.C.
Crystal Cathedral

For You, And You Alone

All the ways You work in my life are amazing, God,
And I want to thank You for taking the time;
Sins can be so heavy and disgraceful,
I'm so grateful You've forgiven me mine.

I know that at times I'm not always attuned,
And that I let the world suck the life out of me;
And I confess to getting sidetracked,
From the heir you intended me to be.

Faults or flaws—You love me nonetheless,
You're the most unconditional love of all;
On the road of life, I fail, stumble and trip,
Always You catch me the moment I fall.

God, please help me live a Christian life,
To make Your perfect will my own;
Please help me dedicate my life to You,
And live it for You, and You alone.

—Sarah Erdman, 16

Letter from a Youth Counselor

Dear Readers,

In teaching and counseling young people over the years as a high-school educator, I've discovered that many of you are looking for guidance in your search to find meaning for your existence, someone or something to believe in, and a certain stability that helps you to decide on your actions in an ever-changing world. Many seek answers to life's questions in wonderful, creative and imaginative ways, while others do so in unhealthy ways, including escape through alcohol and drugs, sexual relationships, a pursuit of popularity and membership in groups, including gangs, which are only distractions that waylay the finding of true fulfillment. How can you find lasting happiness and fulfillment? The answer was given, in fact, to an ancient people, but it can still work for you, a young adult living in very new times. Surprisingly, understanding "the past" can help you make sense of "the now."

About 3,400 years ago, a man descended from a mountain in the desert in the Sinai Peninsula with what would become the legal foundation, not only for the Israelites, but for much of Western culture. When God gave Moses the Decalogue or "ten words"—also known as the Ten Commandments—it was an establishment of God's moral law, but He didn't say, "This only pertains to the

Israelites." These laws were designed for all humankind's benefit. They were given by the Creator to provide order, meaning and purpose for everyone throughout His creation—then, and for all time to come. These are not "old and weird laws," but rather, sensible rules that bring order to living, happiness of spirit and solace to the soul. Are you experiencing the blessings of God in your life? Such blessings come from living the Commandments.

You live in a world where many people believe the Ten Commandments are an outdated part of the past. They have made many challenges to our Judeo-Christian heritage in the courts and, piece by piece, are removing these elements from education and public life much like the Israelites of old who broke God's commands and received the consequences of their behavior. For example, in 1980, the United States Supreme Court ruled in *Stone v. Graham* that hanging a passive display of the Ten Commandments in a public school in Kentucky was unconstitutional. The opinion of the Court stated, "This is not a case in which the Ten Commandments are integrated into the school curriculum, where the Bible may Constitutionally be used in an appropriate study of history, civilization, ethics, comparative religion, or the like. Posting of religious texts on the wall serves no such educational function. If the posted copies of the Ten Commandments are to have any effect at all, it will be to induce the young people to read, meditate on, perhaps venerate and obey, the Commandments. However desirable this might be as a matter of private devotion, it is not a permissible state objective under the establishment clause." How do you feel about that— knowing the Ten Commandments cannot hang on the walls, yet other plaques, slogans, inspirational posters, and even pictures of witches (witchcraft is a religion) do?

The court said, in essence, that our founding fathers would not have wanted the Ten Commandments to hang on the wall in a public (government) school because it would establish a religion. Do you agree? This was the decision despite statements by our nation's founding fathers to the contrary. Consider this most important statement by James Madison, who was largely responsible for the design of the Constitution, "We have staked the whole future of American civilization, not upon the power of government, far from it. We have staked the future of all of our political institutions upon the capacity of each and all of us to govern ourselves according to the Commandments of God. The future and success of America is not in this Constitution, but in the laws of God upon which this Constitution is founded."

Have there been negative consequences as a result of removing the Ten Commandments from the everyday places where we can see them and remind ourselves of their place in our lives? You have probably heard all about the shootings at Columbine High School in Littleton, Colorado, in April 1999. In December 1997, in Paducah, Kentucky, a fourteen-year-old boy opened fire on students meeting for prayer before their school day. Five students were killed and three were wounded. This was the same state where the Supreme Court ruled it was unconstitutional to hang the Ten Commandments because the students may, perhaps, obey them. Do you know of any other school shootings? They are numerous. Are these some of the consequences for failure to teach God's principles to our young people?

More recently, in August 2003, a five-thousand-pound granite monument of the Ten Commandments was removed from the rotunda in the Alabama Supreme Court building amidst demonstrations by protestors. U.S. District Judge Myron Thompson of Montgomery had ruled that the monument violated the Constitution's ban on the government endorsement of a religious doctrine. In reality, the Constitution makes no statement to this effect. Again, those who are trying to remove our Judeo-Christian heritage have misused the Constitution. The First Amendment begins, "Congress shall make no law respecting an establishment of religion or prohibiting the free exercise thereof."

Congress did not require the monument to be erected, and there is no religion being established by congressional law. Suspended Supreme Court Chief Justice Roy Moore stated, "It is a sad day in our country when the moral foundation of our laws and the acknowledgment of God has to be hidden from public view to appease a federal judge." If there is any misrepresentation of the Supreme Law of the Land, it is by the justice who made the ruling to have the monument removed. Our first president George Washington said, "Do not let anyone claim the tribute of American patriotism if they ever attempt to remove religion from politics."

And if there is a constitutional ban on the government endorsement of a religious doctrine, then why do government-run schools endorse religions like Secular Humanism, Atheism (yes, it's a religion) and New Age, while the Ten Commandments can't be displayed? Do you see hypocrisy in the so-called teaching of "tolerance" and respect for religious "diversity" in the government-run schools? How many more national tragedies will it take before people realize the importance of teaching the principles found in the Ten Commandments?

Yes, the Ten Commandments are as relevant and important today as ever. In today's world, the Ten Commandments—as always—help us develop values that give meaning and relevance to our lives. They give societies basic guidelines to live by and, if followed, bring happiness and blessings to all. Perhaps more than ever before, young adults need a barometer so as to shape their beliefs and values, to rethink their lifestyles, and to make wise choices that will allow them to receive God's blessings and restore order to a rapidly changing society. How can you take advantage of the principles set forth in "The Decalogue" to make it through the jungle of choices and challenges you face today? For one, you can read the Ten Commandments, meditate on them and follow them. You can support those like Judge Roy Moore who oppose the injustices of so-called "justices." Speak up, vote or run for office when you are of the age to do that, get involved. You can make a difference.

Maybe you aren't familiar with the Ten Commandments. Or maybe you have heard of them, but don't really understand them or put them into practice in your life. This book will be a great help. Here you'll read about the Commandments and God's intent behind each law. You'll get a chance to look at the meaning of each Commandment and the precise ways it applies to your everyday life. And you'll hear from your peers about how they understand the Ten Commandments and have made practical application of them in their own lives. This will be of great help and encouragement as you search for your place in the world and seek an understanding of God's purpose for your life.

I hope and pray that you will seriously consider the significance of the Ten Commandments and see them as a compass for your journey—right now—and throughout your life. You will not be alone on this journey if you allow God to be your Heavenly Father. He has not given these rules for the purpose of taking away your fun. Like a loving parent, He has provided these rules to prevent His children from experiencing negative consequences much like a parent who tells his teenager not to get in the car with someone who is under the influence of alcohol or drugs. God has given rules because of His incredible love for you, His desire that your life not be wasted, and His wish that you might come to know His love. As you'll discover in each Commandment, God reveals something that is important to your well-being. As you will read in this most important book by Bettie B. Youngs, an author you've come to love and trust, you'll uncover what each one is and see how it brings meaning and direction to your life. My sincere desire is that you find true joy in the blessings of God. May God bless you as you begin your journey through each of these God-inspired chapters.

Michael Pichette
educator, Santa Fe Christian Schools
author, *The Great Bundingle Race*

Angels in Our Midst

Angels on the subway
Angels in the park
Angels in a lighthouse
Angels guarding in the dark.

Angels in the taxi
Angels on the train
Angels walking down Main Street
Angels dancing in the rain.

Angels in the bakery
Angels packing bags to go to camp
Angels at the grocery store
Angels on the parking ramp.

Angels singing at a wedding
Angels walking down school halls
Angels playing professional soccer
Angels at the local mall.

Angels doing yoga
Angels teaching at your school
Angels taking photos
Angels swimming in the pool.

Angels working in the office
Angels writing spirit books
Angels cooking a favorite dinner
God's love . . . is everywhere you look!

—**Stephanie Lloyd, 14**

Acknowledgments

There are no words, really, to describe the beauty, power and honor in writing this book. Words do not escape me, however, for appreciating those who in some way were a part of its journey into being. First, to guardian angels Mom and Dad: Thanks for alighting on my shoulders throughout the writing of this book. Angel wings, I see, aren't nearly as clumpy as I'd thought they'd be! Also, to my sisters Judy and Laurel and my brothers Mark and Kevin for the gift of love and fellowship. We drew closer during this book than at any other time in our busy and family-oriented lives—I'd be orphaned without you! Thank you, daughter Jennifer, for always loving me and trusting the journey of growing into who we are. Never do we doubt that God's hand is upon us—individually and collectively. Thank you, God, for that.

I'd also like to thank some very special people who have been an integral part of my own Christian Walk. First, to Lloyd Larsen, a favorite Sunday School teacher from my youth. A total supporter of every human life in our community, Lloyd sat front and center at every congregational member's baptism, confirmation, wedding or funeral. Always, always, Lloyd Larsen was there. A tireless servant of God, his joyful brand of abiding love of God was amazingly simple—and, therefore, potent. Incidentally, Lloyd was also the church custodian, but most of us assumed it was just a front: He simply loved His Lord's people, and there wasn't a moment he didn't find it joyful to support and assist. Lloyd, outside of my mother's example of Christian living, you remain the most powerful example of Christian love I've known.

Thank you to the late—and great!—Pastor Kenneth Torvic (and wife, Alma). Pastor Torvic, a most beloved minister (with the giant-sized hobby of tending to bees!), baptized me as an infant, confirmed me as a teen, married me to my daughter's father (and baptized my daughter!) and, most of all, was a charismatic dynamo who taught me everything a girl could want to know about tending to beehives! This skill—not coincidently—was learned by every young person in our community who began to show signs of an "identity crisis" or appeared to be heading into "a rebellious streak." At such times, Pastor Torvic appeared and whisked that teen away for whatever length of time it took for him to attend to his bees! Thanks for saving "your kids," as you called us, from being grounded by our parents for life, and maybe even sent to reform school! There wasn't a young person in town who didn't want to be like you—and to know and be loved by the God you revered and loved. Thank you for that example.

And to Reverend Schiller and your family, thank you for loving our family as you did. When I saw you yet again at my father's funeral this past spring and listened to your words, your love for us soothed my broken heart. That you came to our community was both a blessing and a miracle. Thank you, God, for always sending us what we need.

A most special thank-you to my publisher, Peter Vegso, founder and president of Health Communications and the new Christian imprint, Faith Communications—its mission being to "cultivate a desire to pursue Christ, grow in faith and share his love with others." Thank you, Peter, for so many opportunities over the years to change the world, in your words, "one reader at a time." Thank you, as well, to the dedicated and talented staff at HCI, most especially those with whom I work most closely: First, to Susan Heim, who on this book is senior editor—and who is, at this writing, expecting twins! I honor your professional skills, Susan, but it is your loving heart that is the real gift. Thank you so very much for the wholeness of spirit that is so very evident in all our discussions and e-mails—and throughout these pages. Thank you to pro Paola Fernandez in public relations for adding wings to this book so that it might take flight and land where it is meant to. Thank you also to Lisa Drucker, Lori Golden, Randee Feldman, Terry Burke, Kelly Johnson Maragni, Tom Sand, Elisabeth Rinaldi, Melissa Zbikowski, Tom Galvin, Kim Weiss, Brian Peluso—as well as to the many others who play an intricate role in transporting this book into the hands and hearts of readers. A special thanks to Nancy Curtis, Rebecca Evans and students at Santa Fe Christian for your influence on this work.

As always, a special thanks to Andrea Perrine Brower and Larissa Hise Henoch for this book and cover design. When I first laid eyes on the cover, my heart melted, and I understood more deeply the task that lay before me. My words had to parallel the spirit of love and yearning expressed in the outstretched arms of the young person lifting her eyes heavenward as if to say as in Psalm 143:10: "Teach me to do your will, for you are my God." Much of the love contained within these pages ascended from the power this cover evoked. Thank you, Larissa and Andrea, for sensing that this particular photo would stir hearts. It did mine.

Thank you to dear friends, John Potenza, Betty Blair, Buzz Gay, Maria Willia, Barb and Denny Metzler, Nancy Chappie, Cheryl Nason Harris, Tom Sharrit, Jenny Hawkins and Roger Norman, who hold my heart and allow me a private self like no others. As always, thank you Heavenly Father for the gift of life, the joy of the journey and the hope of life everlasting.

A Special Word from the Author

For the sake of simplicity and clarity, personal pronoun references to God in this book will be capitalized (i.e., He) while references to the person of Jesus Christ will be lowercased (he). This in no way makes a doctrinal statement, but serves to make clear the distinction between the two entities.

GOD'S TEN COMMANDMENTS— AND YOU

I have set My rainbow in the clouds, and it will be the sign
of the covenant between Me and the Earth.

Gen. 9:13

With love and honor, I welcome you to this book, an exploration of the Ten Commandments and their relevance for you, a young adult living in a time of unprecedented world events. What exciting times! History is in the making—and you're a big part of it. This is a time when you have more individual rights than ever before, yet a time in which the preservation of those rights is at risk. Many of your brothers and sisters the world over have yet to have the oppressions from which they suffer lifted from their shoulders so that they, too, may rightfully lay claim to the freedoms you enjoy, such as religious worship, safety and wellness, or a chance to go about their lives with full opportunities for supporting their families and enjoying their cultural heritage. May we each make it our obligation—and our honor—to always look out for the welfare of others and to safeguard their rights, just as we would our own. Certainly, looking out for others—seeing our brothers and sisters through the eyes of love—is at the heart of God's love.

This is why writing this book is such a privilege. In these pages, you'll get a chance to explore a topic that is also about "safeguarding welfare"—specifically your own—and discover how you can best provide leadership in these history-making times to which you've been born. Throughout these pages, you'll take a walk through each of the Ten Commandments—laws "inscribed by the finger of God" (Exod. 31:18)—and learn *why* and *how* each Commandment specifically guards something that is of the greatest importance to the welfare of every individual. What a paradise we could create here on Earth if we each would do our part.

We're all here for just a short time, really, although the mission we're on is huge. Contrary to our thinking that the world is a big place, it isn't. We can circle it within a day, and we can talk to practically anyone at any time of day or night. The world-place is, as my friend and astronaut Steve Smith describes, "a little planet that from space looks like a tiny blue marble laying on a Band-Aid-sized strip of black felt." Small or not, we're all here—and here for a reason. The mystery of it all unfolds in the laws inscribed by God, a *covenant* entered into between God and His people nearly 4,000 years ago. Do you know the Commandments? Maybe your parents taught them to you as a young child, or you learned them in Sunday school. Maybe this is your first introduction. Or maybe you have some background, but have a personal goal to become more spiritually aware. This book will help you better understand God's love behind each of His Laws and discern how each applies to your everyday experiences. Love of God and love for others are at the core of God's laws.

What Do the Commandments Mean to You?

What do these ancient biblical laws mean to you, a young person living in exciting, yet turbulent, times? Do you think of the Commandments as really old and outdated, or do you see them as incredibly pertinent? How do the Commandments serve you on a daily basis—from the moment you get out of bed, until your jam-packed and stress-filled day of dealing with others and fulfilling your obligations and responsibilities is over? How do the Commandments apply to the real-life issues young people face, such as a relationship with a special someone, or getting along with family members, friends, educators, employers and others you meet and greet throughout your day? How do the Commandments provide direction for the decisions you face and define the boundaries for your choices—such as staying healthy and fit, choosing or losing friends, attending college, choosing a career or setting goals for your future? How do the Commandments support you in coping with the problems in life, such as stress, depression, wealth or debt? How do the

Commandments both motivate and sustain you in times of crisis—such as the loss of a loved one, a personal setback, or confronting a disability, even a terminal illness? These are important questions, to be sure.

Do the ancient laws really speak to you?

So, do these ancient laws—written 4,000 years ago—speak to you, a young adult living in today's time? You bet! Certainly this is a time in life in which you're hard at work discovering who you are and where you fit in. You're making some incredibly important decisions about everything from "getting a life," to managing a very full and fast one. From making, keeping and losing friends, to "finding" and believing in yourself, you've got your hands full. And you're beginning to know it—which is why you're starting to wonder about a lot of things. For example, you're willing to learn and follow the "rules" so as to be accepted and fit with your peers—but you also know there is a limit on how far you'll go, on just how much you'll compromise, because you intend to stay true to yourself. But who are you? You're busy uncovering your strengths, talents and interests, knowing how important these are to being all you can be. But what should you do and how will you know if you've chosen correctly? Just when you thought you had all the answers, you discover a mountain of puzzling, even baffling, questions.

It's all part of God's plan.

Finding Your Wings: Do You Feel Hopeful, Optimistic and Invincible?

Up to now, you've been part of a "home family," and while that will always remain your "roots," you're finding your "wings" and discovering just how high and far you can fly. You naturally feel hopeful, optimistic and invincible. If you didn't feel this way, you might never venture into the world, where it awaits—even depends upon—your good will, your love, your youthful strength and energy, and most of all, your help and support. And your love of God.

No doubt about it: Life is unfolding for you and taking on shape. More and more, you're beginning to see yourself as not just a bystander in life, but as an active participant—and maybe even a leader. This, too, is all the more reason you will want to understand the laws—governed by love to God and to our neighbor—and see why God shines a spotlight on showing you the way to a glorious life, one that is pure, strong and victorious.

The "Old" Commandments: Still Relevant in "New" Times

Even though God gave the Ten Commandments thousands of years ago, they're still as relevant today as they were back then. Why? Because, though times have changed, people have not. Science continues to make advances that make our lives easier. Technology has transformed our world. Imagine how astounded the Israelites wandering on foot in the wilderness would have been if they could have seen the way we live today with our electrical conveniences and cars and airplanes and rockets and satellites and computers! However, even though our way of life is totally different, the common needs of people to have safety, shelter and emotional security remain the same. The Ten Commandments speak to us in the same way today as they did to the Israelites many centuries ago. God's voice is still providing the guidance and direction we need to maneuver through life—successfully negotiate its ups and downs, its challenges, frustrations and temptations. Throughout it all, we still can know where "the hand of God is that we might know how to live according to His will."

Why Did God Enter into
a Covenant with His People?

At Mount Sinai (you'll get an overview of what happened there in the next chapter), God entered into a covenant with His people of Israel. *A covenant is a contract that guarantees the fulfillment of what has been promised.* You're probably familiar with the covenant God made with Noah. He put the rainbow in the sky as a sign that if Noah would build the ark and do all that God asked of him, then God would never again send a flood to destroy the Earth: "This is the sign of the covenant which I make between Me and you, and every living creature that is with you, for perpetual generations: I set My rainbow in the cloud, and it shall be for the sign of the covenant between Me and the Earth. It shall be when I bring a cloud over the Earth, that the rainbow shall be seen in the cloud" (Gen. 9:12–14 NKJV). Imagine, the beautiful rainbow comes to us as a promise of protection from our Heavenly Father—how totally cool is that?

At Mount Sinai, God pledged to make the Israelites a holy people whom He would use to bring salvation to all mankind. As a sign of acceptance and in celebration, Moses sacrificed an ox to the Lord, taking its blood and sprinkling it upon the altar. (This particular covenant is called "the blood of the covenant.") The people pledged to trust God and keep His word: "We will do everything the Lord has said; we will obey" (Exod. 24:7). As a sign of "sealing" the covenant, Moses said, "This is the blood of the covenant that the Lord has made with you in accordance with all these words" (Exod. 24:8).

If we ask what moved God to enter into a covenant with His people, there is only one answer—His love. He created us. We are made in His image. We are His heirs. To God, each life—each soul—has eternal value. And so because of His love for us, He teaches us how to live a godly life. When we transgress—when we mess up or go astray—He offers us forgiveness of sin through the Savior, and He leads us to faith in Jesus Christ that we might know eternal life. We are His children. He wants us to return to Him, to live with Him eternally. But God must live in us before He can work through us.

The love that moved God to give us the gospel also moved Him to give us His holy law. God first inscribed His law in the heart of man at creation; later He gave the Ten Commandments at Mount Sinai. We call the law inscribed in our hearts the conscience. "The Gentiles . . . show the work of the law written in their hearts, their conscience also bearing witness" (Rom. 2:14–15 KJV). The conscience is always on the side of what we believe to be right. Unless instructed by the Word of God, the conscience may be on the side of what is wrong because we believe it to be right. In order that we may know what is right, God has given us the written law.

The Commandments—Two Tablets "Inscribed by the Finger of God"

The Bible says that the Commandments were chiseled on the front and back of two stone tablets by God's own hand, "inscribed by the finger of God" (Exod. 31:18). Jesus divided the law into two parts—love for God and love for other people. The first four Commandments teach about love for God, and the last six Commandments address love for our neighbor. In the New Testament, when Jesus is asked which law is most important, he sums them all up into two parts, "Love the Lord thy God with all thy heart, and with all thy soul, and with all thy mind. This is the great and first Commandment. And the second is like unto it, thou shalt love thy neighbor as thyself" (Matt. 22:37–39 KJV).

As we learn in Romans 13:10, "Love is the fulfillment of the law." The purpose of the law is threefold:

To teach His people how to live. "The Commandment

is a lamp; and the law is light" (Prov. 6:23 KJV). We're born here on Earth, but we're not without direction on how to live here. Through the word of His Commandments, our Heavenly Father takes us by the hand, inviting us to walk through life together *with* Him.

To teach us that we are not perfect—we sin. Yes, we try to be good and decent people, but our hearts are not as pure as God would like. The Commandments provide the baseline for what is "perfect," and so by comparing ourselves against each standard (i.e., "do not steal"), we know where we stand in God's eyes. If we are off base, our conscience accuses us and we know we've done wrong. "Through the law comes knowledge of sin" (Rom. 3:20 RSV).

To direct us to Christ. When we realize we have much to do in perfecting our nature, we try to do better. But even when we put all our willpower into the task of improving ourselves, we will be unable to produce the purity of heart that God asks of us in His law. Only forgiveness can bring peace to our conscience. Forgiveness of sin is the gift of Jesus Christ. "The law was put in charge to lead us to Christ" (Gal. 3:24).

In Each Commandment, God Guards Something That Is of Great Importance to Our Welfare

In much the same way that a loving parent provides rules so as to look after the safety and happiness of his child, so does our loving Heavenly Father provide rules—laws—for His people. To this end, the Commandments are loving, not limiting. *In each Commandment, God guards something that is of the greatest importance to our welfare.* Because each is a guideline for the way we should live, each addresses what we MUST do and MUST NOT do.

Each Commandment then, is a blueprint, a cornerstone used to govern our behavior. Even aside from the spiritual aspect, each is perfectly formulated "common sense," directing us as to how to live in peace, harmony and safety with each other. They are the basis for moral and spiritual conduct, as well as the foundation of peace and prosperity for the individual and for the entire world, both then and now—and for always.

Can You Recite the Ten Commandments from Memory?

How familiar are you with the Ten Commandments? Can you recite them from memory? Take a moment and write out each one.

1st Commandment: _____

_____

2nd Commandment: _____

_____

3rd Commandment:_____

_____

4th Commandment: _____

_____

5th Commandment: _____

_____

6th Commandment: _____

_____

7th Commandment: _____

_____

8th Commandment: _____

_____

9th Commandment: _____

_____

10th Commandment: _____

_____

Throughout the coming chapters, you'll get a chance to examine each of the Commandments in depth, but here they are, listed in the order in which God delivered them to us.

God's Ten Commandments (Exod. 20:1–17)

1. *I am the Lord your God. . . . You shall have no other gods before me.*

2. *You shall not make for yourself an idol in the form of anything in heaven above or on the Earth beneath or in the waters below. . . .*

3. *You shall not misuse the name of the Lord your God, for the Lord will not hold anyone guiltless who misuses his name.*

4. *Remember the Sabbath day by keeping it holy. . . .*

5. Honor your father and your mother so that you may live long in the land the Lord your God is giving you.

6. You shall not murder.

7. You shall not commit adultery.

8. You shall not steal.

9. You shall not give false testimony against your neighbor.

10. You shall not covet your neighbor's house. You shall not covet your neighbor's wife, or his manservant or maidservant, his ox or donkey, or anything that belongs to your neighbor.

How many of the Ten Commandments did you identify? Hopefully each of the Commandments is so much a part of you that not only can you recite them from memory, but they are deeply integrated into the values by which you live. If you weren't able to recall the Commandments, I encourage you to make that a priority. (You'll find an extra copy of the Commandments in Appendix B in case you'd like to tear that page out and tape it in a handy place so you can more readily commit them to heart.) In this book, you'll have the opportunity to learn more fully how each one applies to your life so that you might come closer to God and live according to His plan for your life. God wants a personal relationship with each and every one of His children. He wants us to know Him personally. To this end, we study His word, and we pray for guidance and direction that we might live according to His laws—the Ten Commandments. Again, these were given out of love for us. But God must live in us before He can work through us. And so our lives must revolve around God if they are to bear fruit for God.

For Christians, the Commandments direct our path that we might know everlasting life. Luckily, we know the "formula" to living life in a way that allows us to feel and be deeply happy and whole. The directive for doing so can be found on that ancient slate of Commandments. The Ten Commandments show us the way—still.

Simple Love

We make His love too narrow
By false limits of our own,
We magnify His strictness
With a zeal He would not own.

If our love were but more simple
If we took Him at His Word,
Then our lives would be less complicated
And we'd know the sweetness of our Lord.

—Arlene B. Burres

MOUNT SINAI: WHAT HAPPENED ON THE MOUNTAIN?

. . . I carried you on eagles' wings . . .

Exod. 19:4

Whe you think about the Ten Commandments, what's the first thing that comes to mind? Is it the movie with the commanding image of actor Charleton Heston as Moses, parting the Red Sea or holding the emblazoned stone tablets high above his head? It's an exciting movie to be sure, and it characterizes a good bit of the amazing history surrounding this most defining moment in time. Still, if you haven't already done so, you'll want to read Exodus 20 for yourself so that you get the full story!

Mount Sinai and the Ten Commandments

You'll read that it was up on Mt. Sinai that God gave the Ten Commandments to Moses. But to better understand the gravity of what happened at Mount Sinai, it's important to know what events led up to it. The Israelites had been taken into slavery in Egypt, and God called a man named Moses to deliver them—to bring them out. God empowered Moses to stand against the Pharaoh (Ramses II), and He sent plagues upon Egypt to convince Pharaoh that he must allow God's people to leave. When the Israelites finally were given permission to leave and had started on their journey, the Egyptians changed their minds and gave chase. That's when the incredible event of the parting of the Red Sea took place. The Israelites walked through the sea on dry ground and then, when the Egyptians got into the riverbed, the invisible dam broke, and the Egyptians drowned.

You'd think the Israelites would have been so awestruck by what God did that they'd live the rest of their lives in joyous thanksgiving, but not so. They got out into the desert and complained; they wanted to go back to Egypt, for at least there they had food to eat. So God gave them fresh, heavenly food (manna) every morning. But when they grew tired of the manna, they complained again.

Three months after they left Egypt, they arrived at Mount Sinai. God told Moses to tell the people: "You yourselves have seen what I did to Egypt and how I carried you on eagles' wings and brought you to Myself. Now if you obey Me fully and keep My covenant, then out of all nations you will be My treasured possession" (Exod. 19:4–5). God also told Moses that in three days He would come to the top of the mountain and the people should be ready. At the appointed time, God arrived with thunder, lightning, a trumpet blast that grew louder and louder, and a cloud of smoke that covered and billowed off the top of Mount Sinai like a furnace. The mountain trembled, and so did the Israelites! It must have been spectacular!

24/7—for Forty Days . . . and Forty Nights!

Moses then went up on the mountain as God instructed and stayed for forty days and forty nights. While he was there, God inscribed the Ten Commandments. The Bible says that the Commandments were chiseled on the front and back of two stone tablets by God's own hand—"inscribed by the finger of God" (Exod. 31:18). God gave the Commandments so He could enter into this covenant with the Israelites. As you'll recall from the last chapter, a covenant is a contract that guarantees the fulfillment of what has been promised.

At Mount Sinai, God entered into a covenant with His people of Israel. He pledged Himself to be their God and to make them a holy people whom He would use to bring salvation to all mankind. As a sign of acceptance and celebration, Moses sacrificed an ox to God, taking its blood and sprinkling it upon an altar. And so this covenant sealed with blood is called the "blood of the covenant." The people pledged themselves to trust God and keep His word: "All that the Lord has said we will do, and be obedient" (Exod. 24:3–8). As a sign of "sealing" the covenant, Moses said, "This is the blood of the covenant which the Lord has made with you according to all these words" (Exod. 24:8).

An Outraged Moses Breaks the Tablets . . . and God Calls Him Back

Meanwhile, at the foot of the mountain, the Israelites already were abandoning God. They gathered all their gold, melted it down and created a calf—to which they bowed down and worshipped. Can you believe their foolishness? Understandably, when Moses came down off the mountain carrying the tablets, he was so outraged that he threw the tablets down and broke them. Then God called Moses back to the mountain. It's hard to tell who was more angry—God or Moses—but Moses pleaded with God to give the people another chance.

God said to Moses, "The Lord, the compassionate and gracious God, slow to anger, abounding in love, and faithfulness, maintaining love to thousands, and forgiving wickedness, rebellion, and sin. . . . I am making a covenant with you" (Exod. 34:6–7, 10). So God forgave the people for abandoning him and again chiseled the Ten Commandments on two new stone tablets. "When Moses came down from Mount Sinai with the two tablets of the Testimony in his hands . . . his face was radiant because he had spoken with the Lord" (Exod. 34:29). At first, seeing the radiance, the people were afraid of Moses, but when he reassured them, they came to him and he gave them the covenant that God had established.

A Wooden Chest Overlaid and Lined with Gold Is Created to Store the Stone Tablets

After Moses gave God's message to the people, he built a wooden chest overlaid and lined with gold—as per God's specific instructions (Exod. 25:10–22)—and placed the tablets in this chest. Because the Israelites had not yet claimed the land that God had promised them, they carried the precious box with them wherever they went. They called the chest and tablets the *Ark of the Covenant* or the *Ark of the Testimony* because it represented God's covenant to be their God and His promise to dwell with them.

What Happened to the Tablets After Mount Sinai?

Did you ever wonder what happened to the tablets after the Israelites left Mt. Sinai? It's a fascinating story. Because God had made the importance of the Ark of the Covenant very clear to them, the people treasured and protected the Ark above everything and everyone; it was a symbol that God was God and that He was watching over them. Even other people knew that God's glory dwelt in the Ark, and the inevitable happened. Another tribe stole the Ark of the Covenant, but they didn't get the results they had hoped for! (See 1 Sam. 4–5.)

The Philistines overthrew the Israelites and captured the Ark of the Covenant. Thinking they had the ultimate power, they took the gold-lined chest bearing the tablets to their temple and placed it beside the statue of their god Dagon. Funny thing—the next morning Dagon was facedown! The Philistines righted the worthless statue only to find it again facedown and broken the next morning. I think we could surmise that Dagon was bowing down to the one, true God! But their trouble was just beginning. Next, the people of Ashdod were afflicted with tumors, so, not surprisingly, the leaders had a meeting. They decided that having the Lord's Ark wasn't a good thing, so they unloaded it by moving it to Gath.

The Lord's hand was heavy on them, as well, and the people of that city, both young and old, were also afflicted with an outbreak of tumors. So the people of Gath moved the Ark to a third city. The people of Ekron fared no better. Actually, they already had heard the rumors of the troubles the other towns had endured when in possession of the golden chest and weren't at all happy to see the Ark of the Covenant coming their way. God was consistent; many people in Ekron died, and the rest were afflicted with, you guessed it, tumors and destruction. Not surprisingly, the Philistines were beginning to get the picture that the God of Israel was thoroughly ticked-off that they had stolen His Ark!

The Trick That Didn't Work Out . . .

So the Philistines devised a little experiment. They placed the Ark on a cart drawn by two oxen and sent it toward the Israelite camp. Complicating the experiment, each of the oxen had a calf that the Philistines locked up. Because it's completely abnormal for a mother ox to deliberately walk away from her offspring, they would know that the God of Israel was, indeed, the one and only God if the oxen went against all nature and traveled with the Ark away from their calves.

Imagine the Philistines standing by the road and watching expectantly as they put their experiment into motion. The oxen traveled straight for the Israelite camp and never looked back. The Israelites were thrilled beyond measure to have their beloved Ark returned, and the Philistines were just as happy to be rid of it! It just goes to show that God was obviously very protective of His stone tablets bearing His Ten Commandments. They were the representation of His covenant with His people, and no one was going to change the plan.

The Ark of the Covenant (Here's Where Indiana Jones Fits into All This)

When the Israelites built the temple in Jerusalem, the gold-lined chest holding the precious stone tablets was placed in the inner sanctum, the most holy place in the temple. It was called the Holy of Holies because God's presence and glory dwelt in that place. On penalty of death, no one could enter except the high priest who went in once a year to offer sacrifices for the atonement of sins. The Ark of the Covenant was there in the Holy of Holies until the Babylonians destroyed the temple in 586 BC. After that, the Ark of the Covenant disappeared and, to this day, its whereabouts are a mystery. Obviously, there is much speculation among scientists, archeologists and historians as to what happened to the beautiful chest. Many think it may still be buried under the foundation of what once was the temple (under what is now the Muslim-controlled Dome of the Rock), but so far, it has not been uncovered. Does this all sound a little familiar? Maybe you know the Bible story, or maybe you saw Indiana Jones looking for the Ark of the Covenant in the movie *Indiana Jones and the Last Crusade*. Hollywood theatrics aside, it's a fascinating thought that the Ark may still exist, isn't it?

This, of course, is just a thumbnail sketch of the history of the amazing tablets. You can read the Book of Exodus and 1 Samuel 4–6 to get the whole story. One thing is for sure, you'll not find a story anywhere half as interesting!

So the actual tablets have disappeared, but their message is still the cornerstone of human civilization. Simply amazing.

Ancient Freedom

To live a life of joy and freedom,
It's the Commandments you must obey.
They're so much more than ancient words,
They're the rules for work and play.

To live a life of joy and freedom,
Let God walk with you throughout your day.
Then relationships become a privilege
Because you've allowed your will His way.

To live a life of joy and freedom,
When challenging times lead you astray,
Know that Jesus knows your struggles,
Just call on him, listen, read and pray.

To live a life of joy and freedom,
Dare to go beyond what others say.
Yes, it takes courage to live beyond the limits,
Do you really want it any other way?

—Mandy Pohja, 17

THE FIRST
COMMANDMENT

I am the Lord your God. . . . You shall have no other gods before me.

Exod. 20:2–3

I n the previous section, you reviewed the events leading up to the historically monumental "inauguration" of the Commandments. In a most spectacular display of dramatics (which to date, no rock group has been able to upstage!), God "descended to the top of Mount Sinai and called Moses to the top of the mountain. So Moses went up" (Exod. 19:20). The rest is history: Moses went up on the mountain where God gave him the Ten Commandments—His laws for moral and spiritual conduct and the foundation for peace and prosperity for His children. The Scripture goes like this: "When the Lord finished speaking to Moses on Mount Sinai, He gave him the two tablets of the Testimony, the tablets of stone inscribed by the finger of God" (Exod. 31:18). What a beautifully touching image!

In a nutshell, the Commandments are a covenant—an agreement—basically saying, "My part is that I'll be your God and I'll take care of you and provide direction as to how you must conduct yourselves—in mind, body and spirit—down here on Earth (via the Commandments). Your part is to live according to these laws, which are essentially governed by love for God and love for your neighbor."

So that we might know, trust and listen to this direction, God establishes His leadership right off the bat. In the first Commandment, we learn exactly WHO is in charge of things. God starts by introducing himself, "I am the Lord your God" . . . and then issues this foreboding command: "You shall have no other gods before me." In this powerful first law, God establishes right up front that HE—and only He—is God. Not only is He God, but He is *our* God, and we are to put Him first and foremost in our lives. We are to revere, love and trust Him above all things.

In each of His Commandments, God guards something that is of supreme importance to our lives. In this Commandment, God is guarding the single most important prized possession we humans ever will have: *God's love.* The first Commandment, then, reassures us there is One on High, an almighty and omnipotent force—God—whose love for us is beyond any kind of love and magnificence we humans can possibly imagine. It outshines and outlasts any love we ever could hope to have here on Earth—including the abiding and unconditional lifelong love of our parents, or the romantic and serving love of a soul mate by our side throughout our lives. God's love is far greater than love we will experience here on Earth, even though some people here will love us dearly. What an awesome knowing!

God is revere-worthy, love-worthy and trust-worthy. Upholding the first Commandment shows that we revere, love and trust God, and love our "neighbors" as God loves us.

Is God's First Commandment Still Relevant Today?

It's easy to see how when the Earth was so new and people were just beginning to populate villages and towns that rules would be needed. Much like we study for a driver's test to understand road safety, or review classroom rules on the first day of school, rules are necessary for the benefit of all. That Commandments were needed in ancient times to teach everyone the rules—we can see the logic in that. That in the beginning God would need to teach everyone about Himself—"I am the Creator, Master of the Universe, and your Heavenly Father"—is also reasonable. So the first Commandment was definitely relevant then.

But that was then, and this is now, right? The Bible and God's Word have been around for nearly 4,000 years. Christianity has withstood the test of time. We know there is a God (even if He is defined and described in different ways). How, then, does the first Commandment speak to us today? That trillions of people on the Earth haven't yet figured out how to bridge differences of race, color, creed or lifestyle, let alone learned how to live in peace, provides insight, doesn't it? We live in a time in which our days are so chock-full of activities that we have to "power walk," "speed-read" and "multitask" to get things done, accepting as normal our frenetic lifestyles—even though they leave us "burned-out," "brain-dead" and "stressed-to-the-max."

Do we need God when we can entertain ourselves around the clock; conference via satellite anywhere in the world; and talk with our friends by cell phone, even while sending them a snapshot of our latest sweetie or of the dog eating our homework? Do we need God when we can consult with the latest "how-to" guru who can inform us of the recent trends in thinking or values now in vogue? Do we need God when we can get a prescription to regulate our hormones, moods or self-esteem? What do you think? In what ways does God's ancient first law speak to you, a young adult living in a multicultural, fast-paced and high-tech time?

As Christians, We Believe with All Our Hearts That Our Lives Have a Specific Purpose

God knew that our lives would be a battlefield of challenges, but He also knew our hearts. We are made to love God, and we must remember that we were created because of God's love. And so God speaks to us in our hearts and listens to our hearts. He knows that it is in the heart where battles are won and lost. God wants us to find our way to Him, which is why He created a longing for Him in our hearts. Keep in mind that God is our Heavenly Father, and we are His children. He created us in His image. Like a parent, He wants to guide us, to instruct us on how to live our lives. He knows the rules because He created them.

He knows us well, too. He knows we will stumble and fall; He knows we will continue the search. For that we are destined: We each have a mission, a divine purpose for our lives.

And just what might that be? An important premise—one that we Christians believe with all our hearts—is that there is a reason for our being. This ideal is rooted in faith, felt in our hearts, expressed in our joy and lived in our actions daily. What do you believe? Is there a purpose for your life—a divine reason for your time here on Earth? Take a moment now to ponder this question on page 46, then finish reading this chapter.

Is There a Divine Purpose for Your Being, or Is Life Not Much More Intentional Than, Say, a Blade of Grass?

What do you think is the purpose of *your* life? Is it to clean your room, go to school, get your homework done, go to church, go to college, get a job, get married, raise a family, go to work daily, and then retire? And then what? Is the purpose of our lives about the roles we create for ourselves and then go about fulfilling? Or is there more? The Bible tells us we are made in God's image. If your birthright is that of an heir, you're in God's family—which means you have a legacy to fulfill. Do you believe that your life has the divine purpose of being an heir to God's kingdom—or that it has not much more intention than, say, a blade of grass or a mushroom?

For Christians, the answer is simple and straightforward: We are on a journey. We are trying to find our way home. Home to God. We want eternal life with our Father, our Heavenly Father, our Creator. How do we get there? Figuratively and literally, we are to follow the map we'll find in God's "textbook" for the great school of life (the Bible). Here we will find clear and concise directions (the Commandments) for how to live our lives God's

way. The Commandments are God's "streetlight" for us to follow; they are God's "rules" for our play and for our work. The
Commandments give the answers to the battlefield of challenges
we all face in our lives—and in them we find eternal life.

Are You on a Journey— or Chasing After the Wind?

Would you characterize your life as routine, too busy, even
boring? Do you feel tired and drained, as though you need to
"get a life"? That can happen, especially if we lose sight of the
reason why we're here, the reason we have life in the first place.
Hopefully, you believe it is your "earthly work" to be filled with
His Holy Spirit, and all services and duties rendered in your lifetime are a "reasonable response" to being loved by God. If so,
then your life has meaning, purpose and direction. Are you following God's spotlight shining the way to a glorious life that is
pure, strong and victorious? That is the reason for the journey.
But what if we get lost or detoured along the way—what if "life
happens"? This will happen to some of us, but it will be through
no fault of God's directions. As we learn in Psalm 119:105, "Your
Word is a lamp to my feet and a light for my path."

So the Commandments offer direction. You see, God does not
put us here on this Earth and say, "There you go. Have a nice trip.
Hope to see you later." Like a newborn, we need daily care, and
we need to be instructed on how "life works." God knows this.
The Commandments offer the guidelines for how "life works,"
starting off with the assurance we find in the first Commandment
in which God basically says, "Hey, I'm your daddy. Listen to My
voice, that you might know Me. Listen to My guidance, that you
might learn how to walk. Feel My love, that you might truly love
yourself and others. Hear My Word, that you might share it with
your siblings—all over the Earth. I'm here for you—all you have

to do is call on Me. I am your Father. I am the Lord your God. Unchanging, always and forevermore."

And so God sets about parenting us. He directs that a relationship with Him is to be the focus, in fact, the very core, of our lives. We are to be firmly rooted in God. The command is clear: God is to be #1 in our lives—all the time and in all ways. Scripture tells us that we are not to place concern for livelihood before Him, nor the acquisition of money or material possessions, not fame or popularity—or anything else. Why? Because "chasing" after these things would serve only to separate us from God, and God knows no amount of "stuff" can bring us happiness. As we learn in Ecclesiastes 2:4–17 (RSV): "I made great works; I built houses and vineyards for myself. . . . I bought male and female slaves. . . . I had also . . . great herds and flocks. . . . I also gathered for myself silver and gold and the treasures of kings. . . . I kept my heart from no pleasure. . . . Then I considered all that my hands had done and the toil I had spent doing it . . . all was vanity and a striving after wind. . . . So I hated life . . . for all is vanity and a striving after wind."

Do You Place God First and Foremost in Your Life?

Our Heavenly Father knows us—after all, He made us—and He knows there is only one thing that satisfies our soul: living according to His commandments. All else is fleeting: "Naked a man comes from his mother's womb, and as he comes, so he departs" (Eccles. 5:15). We are to do as Jesus said, "Worship the Lord your God, and serve Him only" (Matt. 4:10). We must not idolize anything that detracts us from the purpose of our earthly journey—which is to experience God's love and know His will. If our lives are to have meaning at all, if they are to serve any purpose, then we must live according to the Commandments.

But God must live in us before He can work through us.

And so the first Commandment begins with God's instructions as to what we are to do and not to do to be "heirs" to God. Because we are grateful for this guidance that leads to the path of eternal life, we naturally should revere, love and trust God.

Revere, love and trust: What do these terms really mean?

What Does It Mean to "Revere" God?

We are to revere God. In many instances the Bible says we are to "fear" God. Certainly when God speaks about a consequence for not following a command, there is no doubt about the authoritative voice with which He speaks. Does the notion "to fear God" make God seem a little foreboding? We'd rather think of God as loving and forgiving, but the truth is, we'd better fear Him as well. Consider His words, ". . . I, the Lord your God, am a jealous God, punishing the children for the sin of the fathers to the third and fourth generation of those who hate Me . . ." (Exod. 20:5). If that doesn't make anyone quake, what will? Thankfully, He follows these very words with, ". . . but showing love to a thousand (generations) of those who love Me and keep My commandments" (Exod. 20:6).

To "revere" God means to stand in awe of His power, His authority, His greatness. Jesus said, "All authority in heaven and on Earth has been given to me" (Matt. 28:18). Therefore, to fear God means to acknowledge His authority and to revere His position as the one and only God.

What Would You Think, Do or Say If God Dropped In on You . . . ?

To help you get a sense for the "reverence" we're to have for God, place Him in your presence for a moment. Imagine that God has—without notice—joined you and your family at the dinner table. Or He's decided to pop in at your school and greets you at your locker or takes a seat next to you at lunch. Or maybe He decides to join you at your job and meets up with you by the watercooler. Approaching you, He says in a loving, but most unyielding voice, "Hi. I am the Lord your God—and you're to have no other gods before me." How would you feel? This is God, your Creator. Your Heavenly Father. The one who knew you "even as you were knit together in your mother's womb" (from Ps. 139:13), the One who sits in charge come Judgment Day.

Think back to a time when a teacher (or parent, coach or employer) called you on something because you'd been out of line. How did you feel? Did the fact that you'd been called on by a person in a position of authority get your attention? Did it make you a tad bit "fearful"? No doubt it did. Likewise, God wants us to revere Him, knowing that he is most serious about the Laws He's given us. Take a moment to reflect on God's command in His first law. Only a fool wouldn't "listen up," right? That's what reverence is—the kind of "fear" for which God is deserving.

By the way, the thought of God sitting near you at school or at work isn't all that farfetched because God is always that close to us—every day and in every way. But we let our attention drift. Someone once said, "If God doesn't give you all you deserve, thank Him!" Do all you can to be worthy of God's love.

God promises consequences for all who transgress against His commandments. We therefore should revere Him and not break His laws. As we learn in Galatians 6:7, "Do not be deceived; God cannot be mocked; a man reaps what he sows." But He promises grace and every blessing to all who keep His laws. We should therefore love Him and trust Him, and gladly keep His commandments. And so we find a fearful seriousness in what God says of sin: "The soul who sins is the one who will die" (Ezek. 18:4).

"Fearful seriousness": God does not shy away from reminding us of consequences

God does not shy away from reminding us there are consequences for not obeying the laws He set forth to guide our lives in the direction of fulfilling our purpose. He doesn't just say, "These commandments are to help you live orderly lives and to be able to know what is expected of each person—but it's okay if you do your own thing." Nor does He say, "If some of you want to live by them, good. And if others refuse, that's okay, too."

What would life be like if each of us "did our own thing"— lived in the way we each simply chose to? Would the bullies of the world oppress the meek, timid and shy among us? Yes, and worse. Look around and you'll see it happening all over in our world. God knows this and says that all the laws apply to each and every one of us. If we refuse to obey them, then consequences follow. We should take heed: The agony of an accusing conscience is one form of punishment. Loss of honor, health, friends and property are other forms. Eternal separation from God is the last and worst punishment.

The Bible tells us that even the sins of the fathers come as punishment upon children who hate God. Parents' evil reputation, immorality and other forms of ungodliness are inherited and increased in children who continue in the same evil ways. Thus sin becomes a destructive curse from generation to generation. This is heavy and serious, isn't it? But on the flip side, consider that we also have God's blessings. God shows mercy to us in order to encourage, inspire and enable us to live according to His will. This is how much God loves His children and wants us to return to the fold. If we ask for forgiveness, God forgives. For even the most serious things that we do, if we repent (ask from the bottom of our hearts for God to make us new, whole and pure), He wipes the slate clean. He then makes us a blessing to other people.

The Fear and Love of God Are the Strongest Building Forces in Human Life

God's love is so encompassing that when we ask Him into our lives, He uses our sufferings—our battlefield of challenges—as a means for building up our spiritual lives. Fear and love of God are the strongest building forces in human life, while sin is the greatest destroyer. "We know that to them that love God all things work together for good" (Rom. 8:28).

God's blessings do not stop with the individual, but are in many ways inherited by their children and shared by society. The human family is so closely knit together that we transmit to our children both the fruits of our sins and the blessings of a God-fearing life. "But from everlasting to everlasting, the Lord's love is with those who fear him, and his righteousness with their children's children" (Ps. 103:17). "Godliness has value for all things, holding promise for both the present life and the life to come" (1 Tim. 4:8).

So the Commandments teach us how our Heavenly Father wants us to live. It is a beautiful life, pure, strong, victorious and governed by love to God and to our neighbor. We also have come to realize that the best of us are far from perfect. We have done many things God has forbidden. In addition, we lack the purity of motives, the wholeheartedness and fullness of love that God wants us to demonstrate—and to see in each other. As much as we'd like to think we're simply the best, we all sin and need forgiveness. God provided this forgiveness by sending His Son to die for us and by giving us His Holy Spirit.

So is it really so difficult to accept that a God who grants us our lives and provides for us would not have stiff penalties for those who don't follow His laws? No. What is at stake when we disobey His commands? Nothing less than eternal life.

Revering God—A Word from Your Peers

I know teens who don't believe in God, and I know others who turn to God only when it's convenient for them—like when they're really hurting or stressed. I even know kids with an "I-am-too-cool-to-need-God" attitude, and they roll their eyes when anyone talks about God. And I know teens who think of God in New Age terms—you know, that everything is love, love, love. This is all misguided, as my youth pastor suggested. I know that God watches over me and sees and knows everything I do. So God doesn't need a makeover. He'll always be the same—the same God with the same promises. And that's what's so reassuring about God. He's the same 24/7.

—Carren Amos, 17

I don't have a problem knowing that I'm to have a healthy "fear" of the Lord. I feel this way about my parents (especially when I'm in trouble). And I respect my teachers and coaches; I know that I have to follow prescribed rules or there will be consequences. It's not my prerogative to interpret these rules as to what's handy for me, so why should it be different in my relationship with God? Having "restrictions" is one way I know how much others care about me and are willing to protect me from the big, bad world. I'm okay with rules and boundaries and Commandments. I find them reassuring.

—Leo Wright, 15

The God I know is the One who keeps me from lifting stuff from stores, buying pornography, even from buying and selling drugs to my friends. Knowing that God watches over me each day helps me to get clear about my values and, as a result, to live according to the laws of the land. Really, no matter how "out there" it sounds, if it weren't for rules, I don't know that I'd be a decent person to be around. Would I be afraid if I had to face a judge in a court of law? Absolutely. Am I "afraid" of God? Yeah, I'm afraid of facing God if I've done a lot of bad stuff. You bet. That God has said, "Hey, I'm God and I've set rules and you're to obey them," well, I believe Him. And contrary to some of my friends who don't believe in God or who need God to be all honey-pie and sweet, well, I'm not taking chances.

—Curt Binghman, 16

When I was little, I thought my parents were silly to make me get off my bike and look both ways before crossing the street. When I thought they weren't looking, I'd glance both ways and ride on across. One day I rode out from behind a parked car into the path of a car. The driver braked and swerved, but he still clipped my bike. My leg was broken above my knee, and I had surgery and spent months in a body cast. God didn't break my leg because I disobeyed my parents, but I learned a valuable lesson. To me, that's what fearing the Lord means—to listen and respect. You know, cause, effect; cause, effect; cause, effect. It's a pretty simple equation.

—Debbie Del Guercio, 13

I think of God in terms of a no-nonsense judge. Even though I've never been hauled into court (and don't plan to be!), the thought that I would be facing a judge who has the power to levy a sentence—be it a fine or jail time—scares me to death. It's this fear that keeps me from drinking and driving and doing other illegal—and basically, stupid—stuff. It's just not worth the risk. Likewise, if we don't in some way believe that God has rules for the way we conduct ourselves—if we just all "do our own thing"—if we live as though there are no rules, either in the way we treat others or ask them to treat us in return, then the human race cannot survive. And aside from making daily life work, we have to keep in mind that there will come a day when we're going to die. When that day comes, we're going to stand before the Judge. One of the qualities of God is that He's a God of justice—that's not a flaw; that's part of His perfection. If you want to take your chances that none of this is true, then you are more of a "risk-taker" than I am!

—Kevin Thurman, 18

I have some friends who care more about what others think and say about them than about God's assessment. Whenever I see this, I usually conclude that the person doesn't have a personal relationship with God—because to know God is to measure everything you do and say in relation to what you know God expects. What He expects is pretty clear: The Commandments spell it all out. So in everything, I first ask myself, "What would Jesus do?" I like knowing I have God's guidance. It's amazing how simple and straightforward life gets when I put God first.

—Brad Tomelson, 16

What Does It Mean to "Love" God?

God's love is so much higher and more pure than any human love. God loved us when He created the world and human beings to live in it. God looked down through the ages and knew there would be a "you" and a "me" and even knew us by name. He saw us when we were formed in our mothers' wombs (Isa. 44:2), and He knows us so well that He numbers every hair on our heads. "But the very hairs on your head are all numbered" (Matt. 10:30). Now that is an amazing brand of love!

Let's back up and explore Jesus' role in God's love because it's pivotal in understanding just how much God loves us. In the previous section, you read about Kevin Thurman's sense of God as a judge. Think about standing before a judge in a court of law following a crime or offense that you've committed. The judge is about to hand down your sentence. You probably quake and tremble at the prospect of the verdict you know you deserve. However, instead of reading you the sentence, then slamming down his gavel and dismissing you, the judge looks at you tenderly and says, "I consider you as my child, and you are free to go because someone else paid your penalty." That's the kind of judge God will be when you stand before Him to answer for the choices you've made in your life. That's how much God loves you and me. "This is love, not that we loved God, but that he loved us and sent his Son as an atoning sacrifice for our sin" (1 John 4:10).

If you have accepted that Jesus traded places with you, then your sins are forgiven. God actually sees you as being as sinless as Jesus. That's what happened when he traded places with you. If that weren't enough, God gave you life and sustains it every day. The air you breathe, the food you eat, the clothes you wear, your family, your friends, your ability to learn—are all gifts from God because He loves you. Even if you think something is missing—perhaps your parents are separated or divorced and you don't get to spend as much time with one or both of them as you'd like, or making good grades doesn't come as easily for you as for some others, or you're not as athletic as you'd like—know that God loves you.

Allowing us to struggle is actually a part of God's love for us because our struggles make us stronger. God has a perfect plan for your life, and it doesn't look like anyone else's perfect plan. Yes, it's perfect—even though we humans have a tendency to look around and sometimes wonder why others have it "bigger, better, brighter." You didn't get gypped: Trust that God knows what He's doing. And by the way, if you question any of this, have a heart-to-heart talk with God. Trust that God is waiting to hear from you.

You can understand the concept of divine love through experiencing unconditional love in your own home. Of course, not all of you have that kind of home, and when love is absent or dys-functional, it becomes more difficult to identify with a loving God who cares the same for all of us, but who allows us to choose to love Him. God's love is not based on who we are, what kind of grades we make, how well we fit in or any of the other criteria against which young people sometimes measure them-selves. We're each uniquely made by God expressly for a rela-tionship with Him. That means He wants us to know Him intimately and to love Him because we desire that relationship more than anything. He loves us enough to wait for us to come to Him. He gently prods, but gives us room to decide.

So, what do we do with so great a love? We return it: We fol-low the Commandments He set forth as a code of conduct; we align our will with His; and we trust and believe with all our hearts that God has a plan for our lives and will take care of us.

Loving God—A Word from Your Peers

I'm sure that God loves me, and I trust that He has a plan for me. My response to knowing that God loves me is that I want my love of God to show up in all the things I do, from how I treat each and every one I come across in my daily life, to how willing I am to bring God into the decisions I make every day. Basically, I want others to observe my actions and say, "Oh, what a kind and considerate person he is" and then think, "Hmmm, I'll bet he's this way because he walks with God." I'm not afraid to be a loving person; why should I be afraid to show I love God? So that's the "biggie" as to how I want God to judge me on loving Him—that I lived it for others.

—Brian Burres, 25

I try to be as loving as I can be—even though quite often I have to remind myself to send love along even to those who might like to embarrass me, ridicule or taunt me, or are just plain mean-spirited. I know that God wants me to be a loving person, and to love all that He has created, so I keep working on myself. Being this "loving person" is one way I can witness to others—which I think is a way I witness His love for me.

—Ashley Marx, 17

God's love for me doesn't mean that He drops a cool convertible in my driveway or gives me the answers to an exam I didn't study for or makes all my problems go away. God's love for me means that He'll be by my side as I walk through good times and bad. Although I wouldn't have chosen some of the bad stuff that's happened to me, I can see, looking back, that I'm closer to God and stronger as a result of having struggled with some things. It's all part of the training and a sign that Jesus does love me.

—Noah Johnson, 16

I made some really bad mistakes when I was in tenth grade. I was drinking and doing drugs, I was stealing from family and friends, and then I got pregnant. I was disappointed and embarrassed, and I knew I had let God down. I struggled for a long time to forgive myself, but finally I came to understand that Christ's death on the cross covered it all—there was nothing I could do that Jesus hadn't paid for already. When I accepted that God had forgiven me, then I could forgive myself. And so that enabled me to confront my problems and turn my life around. His forgiveness is amazing. Getting clear on this has made all the difference: I'm not "lost" or rebellious any longer. I don't have to be. I am loved by the Supreme Force in the universe. I walk with my head up because my heart is filled with love. As a result, I have very little to prove these days— which, by the way, shows up in the joy-filled smile I wear.

—MerryLynn Hennessey, 18

What Does It Mean to "Trust" God?

To be trusted is the highest compliment. "Who can I really trust?" is an important question. In the journal section at the end of this chapter, you'll see a question on page 49 that asks you to write down the names of those who have your innermost confidence and trust. Go ahead and do this now, then come back and continue reading.

Was your list long or short? Trust is an important quality, isn't it? It is also one for which the measuring stick is one we keep deep within our hearts. So who can you trust? For sure, we can trust God; He's not going to let us down. As we learn in Psalms 84:11–12: "For the Lord God is a sun and a shield; the Lord bestows favor and honor; no good thing does he withhold from those whose walk is blameless. O Lord Almighty, blessed is the man who trusts in you."

Trust means to depend on, to have faith in, confidence in, security in. Remembering that God sent His Son to die for you, thinking how God has prepared a place for you in heaven so that you can spend eternity with Him, considering how He created you and numbered the hairs on your head, it's a pretty safe jump to expect that you can trust Him with your life, don't you think? A beautiful Scripture on the subject is Proverbs 3:5–6: "Trust in the Lord with all your heart and lean not on your own understanding. In all your ways acknowledge him, and he will make your paths straight."

Our mandate to trust God further clarifies that we are not to "lean on our own understanding." If we trust God and then dictate to Him what we want done, how we want it done and when we want it done, He probably shakes his head and says, "If you trust me, then let Me take care of the what and when and how." He wants us to acknowledge Him in all ways. That means we need to remember that He's God and we're not! Then He'll make our paths straight. That means we can trust Him to remove the obstacles and clear the road because a child of God is coming through—like the following young people have discovered.

Trusting God—A Word from Your Peers

I'm at a crossroads in my life right now. I've got lots of important decisions to make—where I'll go to college, what I will major in and what career that will lead to. I'm really in love with a guy, and we're trying to decide if being engaged is the best and right decision. I know that with the freedom of college we'll both be faced with temptations that we've not had to struggle with before. I could be "crazed" over it, but the best thing for me to do is to put my faith and trust in the Lord—and ask Him to watch over me and the person I love. I can trust that if this relationship is going to survive, it's because God wants it to. I trust that whatever happens, God considers it best and right for me.
—**Kerri Mathis, 18**

God created me, and I turned out okay, so I figure God pretty much has a handle on things. Why should I doubt God? I trust Him. I don't have a reason not to.
—**Micah Forsyth, 12**

A person I thought was a good friend betrayed me. I was really hurt and still struggle with being able to trust anyone again, although I do find comfort in talking with God and asking Him to take away my pain or at least make it bearable. My heart is hurting a lot, so I ask a lot. But just the asking brings great comfort. I can trust the comfort God gives to help me make it through. If I didn't think God could help me in this really tough time, I honestly don't think I could get through it. It's great to know that God is trustworthy, especially since right now I'm having a difficult time believing people are!
—**Kim Sullivan, 16**

When I was fifteen, I had an accident on my three-wheel ATV. I was riding late one afternoon when I lost control going down a hill and ended up being pinned under it. Because I'd ridden to a remote area that was far from home and far from any road or house, I realized that no one would be coming my way anytime soon—although I did yell out for help. Finally, because I had no other hope, I prayed, "God, You've got to help me outta here. I can't do this on my own." Within an hour, I heard the yelping of dogs and the cheery whistle of a local rider passing by. I could tell you of a hundred other incidents that show me that God sees and hears all. Me doubt God? I don't think so!

—Jerry Cordell, 17

I've made plenty of mistakes in my life, the biggest one not realizing that I could trust God. I sort of knew that I could trust Him with the big things—like when we moved and it really wasn't long before I'd found new friends, or like the time when my dad lost his job and then suddenly found an even better and more suitable one. I didn't think a busy God would have time for the little stuff, but I've learned that type of thinking is really about our own small-mindedness. When I find myself all anxious and apprehensive about things, I turn it over to God. God cares, and I trust that.

—Luke Ellis, 16

God Is Revere-Worthy, Love-Worthy and Trust-Worthy

There is no question about God's willingness to be our God, or of His being worthy of our praise and thanksgiving. Do you talk with God daily? Do you take your joys, sadness, problems and questions to Him? If not, why not? If you trust Him with your daily comings and goings, why not your life? Be willing to put God first in your life. Ask Him to help you have a glorious life, one that is pure, strong and victorious.

YOUR PERSONAL JOURNAL

In what ways does God's first Commandment apply to your life today? In what ways is it still relevant?

_____

_____

_____

_____

_____

_____

_____

Think about your lifestyle. In what ways do you break the first Commandment?

_____

_____

_____

_____

In what ways do you uphold the first Commandment?

_____

_____

_____

_____

_____

_____

In the first Commandment we're told to love God above all else. Do you think this includes even our parents, siblings and grandparents? What about ourselves—are we to love and think about God even before we think of ourselves? Explain.

_____

_____

_____

_____

_____

_____

Have you made God the Lord of your life—is He at the center of all that you do? If not, why not? If so, do you recall the day and time of making that decision?

_____

_____

_____

_____

_____

_____

Do you consider having heart-to-heart talks with God on a daily basis one way you can show that you revere, love and trust God? Explain.

_____

_____

_____

_____

_____

_____

Do you consider God's love as the single most "prized possession" you have? In what way is having God's love a "blessing" to you?

_____

_____

_____

_____

_____

_____

The first Commandment reassures us that we are not without "leadership." Do you ever think of God in this way—as a leader? In what ways does God offer leadership in your life? Explain.

_____

_____

_____

_____

_____

_____

The first Commandment asks us to revere God. In what ways do you consider God "revere-worthy"?

_____

_____

_____

_____

_____

_____

_____

The first Commandment asks us to love God. In what ways do you consider God "love-worthy"?

_____

_____

_____

_____

_____

_____

The first Commandment asks us to trust God. In what ways do you consider God "trust-worthy"?

_____

_____

_____

_____

_____

_____

Do you think from time to time we need to remind ourselves that God is to be first and foremost in our lives? Why do you think we forget?

_____

_____

_____

_____

_____

_____

Do you believe that people are content when God is at the center of their lives, but feel loneliness and a certain emptiness inside without Him? In what way is this true for you?

_____

_____

_____

_____

_____

Do you think of your life as a "battlefield of challenges"? Explain.

_____

_____

_____

_____

_____

_____

Christians believe with all their hearts that their lives have a specific purpose. Do you believe there is a purpose for your life, a reason for your being? If so, what is your purpose?

_____

_____

_____

_____

_____

Do you consider yourself to be a Christian? How would others know you are a "God-centered" person?

_____

_____

_____

_____

_____

Do you have friends or know someone who is an atheist (a nonbeliever)? How is that person's life different from your own (because of their lack of faith in God)?

_____

_____

_____

_____

_____

As we learn in Ecclesiastes 2:4–17 (RSV): "I made great works; I built houses and vineyards for myself. . . . I bought male and female slaves. . . . I had also . . . great herds and flocks. . . . I also gathered for myself silver and gold and the treasures of kings. . . . I kept my heart from no pleasure. . . . Then I considered all that my hands had done and the toil I had spent doing it . . . all was vanity and a striving after wind. . . . So I hated life . . . for all is vanity and a striving after wind." What does this Scripture mean to you?

_____

_____

_____

_____

_____

_____

_____

In what ways are you "striving after wind"?

_____

_____

_____

_____

_____

_____

_____

_____

What does this Scripture mean to you? "Naked a man comes from his mother's womb, and as he comes, so he departs" (Eccles. 5:15).

_____

_____

_____

_____

_____

_____

In many instances the Bible says we are to "fear" God. What does it mean to "fear" God? In what ways do you "fear" God?

_____

_____

_____

_____

_____

How would you react if God suddenly appeared at your side, such as when you were standing in line at the movies with your friends or eating lunch in the school cafeteria? Would it scare you? Or would you feel humbled, honored and joyous to meet your Creator? Explain.

_____

_____

_____

_____

_____

_____

If God personally came to you and said, "I am the Lord your God. I want you to put Me first and foremost in your life. You're to have no other gods before Me," how would that make you feel? What would you do or say in response?

_____

_____

_____

_____

_____

_____

To be trusted is one of the highest forms of compliment. Who do you trust with all your heart? Write down everyone you can think of and then, next to each name, tell why each is deserving of your utmost confidence.

_____

_____

_____

_____

_____

_____

"Do not be deceived; God cannot be mocked; a man reaps what he sows" (Gal. 6:7). What does this Scripture mean to you?

_____

_____

_____

_____

_____

Has God ever given you a consequence for something you did or didn't do? What was it? How do you know it was God who was levying the consequence?

_____

_____

_____

_____

_____

_____

What would the world be like if each of us "did our own thing"—lived in the way we each simply wanted to? Explain.

_____

_____

_____

_____

_____

_____

Do you believe that "the agony of an accusing conscience" is a form of punishment? Explain.

_____

_____

_____

_____

_____

Fear and love of God are the strongest building forces in human life, while sin is the greatest destroyer. Explain what you think this means.

_____

_____

_____

_____

_____

_____

_____

_____

Think for a moment about your life and the way you've been living it up to now. Now consider standing before God and answering for the choices you've made. What do you consider your greatest "grievance" (sin) for which you hope God will pardon you? Do you think God wants you to make amends for all the ways you've sinned in this lifetime? Have you already talked with God about such things? Why or why not?

_____

_____

_____

_____

_____

_____

_____

_____

_____

"Trust in the Lord with all your heart and lean not on your own understanding; in all your ways acknowledge him, and he will make your paths straight" (Prov. 3:5–6). What does this Scripture mean to you?

_____

_____

_____

_____

_____

_____

_____

If God is not first in your life right now, but you want Him to be your #1 priority, in what ways would you have to change? What would you have to do differently? Are you willing to do that because you revere, love and trust God?

_____

_____

_____

_____

_____

_____

_____

In what ways would the world be different if everyone upheld God's first Commandment?

_____

_____

_____

_____

_____

_____

_____

_____

In what ways would the world be different if *you* upheld God's first Commandment?

_____

_____

_____

_____

_____

_____

_____

How can you keep from growing complacent about upholding God's first Commandment?

_____

_____

_____

_____

_____

_____

The Color of My Creator

When I think of the Creator
I immediately think of color . . .
All those interesting arrangements of white clouds
And the way He splashed the sky with so many hues of blue,
And dyed the sea an aqua green
Touching it up with rippling waves of midnight and navy.
When I think of the Creator
I immediately think of color . . .
And the way He fashioned so many artsy trees
With sturdy trunks and wiry brown limbs
Then clothed them in exotic and shapely leaves of green.
He didn't have to sprinkle
The hummingbird's egg with turquoise—but He did.
What obliged Him to give the sun its golden hue?
The Earth could have been bland,
We would have known no difference.
But our Father chose to color the world . . .
Spice it up with hundreds of interesting faces and places
Perhaps it was to enjoy our reaction
When we felt the sun warm to our skin,
Or breathed in the sweet scent of a lovely rose,
When we knew our heart had fallen in love,
Or noticed the teensy paws of a newborn kitty.
Why did You color the world as You did, God?
Was there a rhyme or reason?
Or was it because You love Your children so much
You simply couldn't help Yourself
From creating a world of beauty
That we might know the splendor of Your love.
It's just a reminder, isn't it . . .
That we belong to You.

—**Jennifer Stripe, 17**

THE SECOND
COMMANDMENT

You shall not make for yourself an idol in the form of any-
thing in heaven above or on the Earth beneath or in the
waters below. You shall not bow down to them or serve
them. . . .

Exod. 20:4–5

In the first Commandment God introduced Himself ("I am the Lord Your God") and instructed us to place our love of Him *above all things.* Having established this foundation, God then orders through the second Commandment that we have but *one* God. We are explicitly forbidden to *make* or *serve* idols—of any kind—regardless of what we find attractive, desirable or honorable in high or low places. We are to pursue God with the clarity of single-minded focus.

As with all the Commandments, God guards something that is of great importance to our welfare. In the previous Commandment it was letting us know with total certainty that GOD IS GOD—the real thing, the one and only. In this second Commandment, God is guarding His relationship between Him and us—His children. We are commanded NOT to place any-thing—figuratively or literally—before Him. Why? Because doing that would interfere with our knowing and loving God in the way He intends. Anything that comes between God and us could separate us from Him. If we place the love of our parents, a boy- or girlfriend, brothers or sisters, friends, the attainment of goals—or anything else—as more important than a relationship with Him, then we may never understand the purpose of our lives, the "why-are-we-here" question, which Psalm 143:10a clarifies as: "Teach me to do your will, for you are my God." Obeying the second Commandment shows that we revere, love and trust God, and we love our "neighbors" as God loves us.

God is serious that we see this law as essential: After telling us that we must not bow down to idols or in any way serve them,

God tells us the ramifications should we not heed his law: "I, the Lord your God, am a jealous God, punishing the children for the sin of the fathers to the third and fourth generation of those who hate Me" (Exod. 20:5). Yes, this sounds harsh. Many young adults reject this facet of God, but they shouldn't.

God does levy consequences for those who transgress His Commandments, and we therefore should have a serious fearfulness about upholding them. And remember this: God promises grace and every blessing to all who keep and uphold the Commandments. We therefore should love and trust Him, and gladly keep His Commandments. And so we find a *fearful* seriousness in what God says of the punishment of sin: "The soul who sins is the one who will die" (Ezek. 18:4). And in Galatians 6:7, "Do not be deceived; God cannot be mocked; a man reaps what he sows." God gives more space to this Commandment than to any of the others, so it must be important to *Him*. Therefore, we can assume that it better be important to us.

Is God's Second Commandment Still Relevant Today?

In what ways does this ancient Commandment have relevancy for our lives today? In a time when "extreme" is the standard and "manifesting" is but a dial tone away, how can we keep God at the center of our lives and need Him more than anything or anyone else? Do we need to be concerned that in a time when anything and everything is within our reach—from fast food to fast cars; from Internet chat rooms to cell phones capable of taking and sending pictures; and, when travel options include boarding a Citation 10 (the fastest plane next to the Concorde) or reserving a seat on the next trip to the moon—that many of God's children would rather play with their "toys" than focus on the lesson in the second Commandment? From screen idols to American Idols to teen idols, can the second Commandment help us decide who is the best of the best, the winner, the "one and only"?

Are You "Good to Go" on the Second Commandment?

Do you think this Commandment has relevance in your life? Where is God on your list of priorities? In what ways do the things you desire and to which you aspire take priority over your time and need for God? Take a moment right now to think about these questions. Make a list of the priorities in your life.

In making your list, what did you discover? Was it clear that God is at the center of your life? Or did your list reveal that it's time for you to have a talk with God and ask Him to help you realign your priorities, to make Him number one again? Are there any "idols" in your life that move God out of His "Head Honcho" spot? Or maybe you feel as sixteen-year-old Colin Long does, that you're "good to go" on this Commandment. In his words, "I'm 'good to go' on the second Commandment. I don't go around carving golden calves to worship; I don't belong to a cult; and I don't think of any rock star as being more cool than my dad. So God can't fault me for not upholding the second Commandment!" How do you feel about Colin's assessment of his being "good to go" with God? Is he "good to go"—or do you think God's intent behind His commandment requires more scrutiny? How about you? Do you need to renew your relationship with God as being your first and foremost priority?

God Knows Our Nature; He Knows We Need Leadership and Inspiration

Why do you suppose God carefully and thoroughly clarifies His intent behind this second law? Maybe one reason is because

God *knows* our nature—He knows that it is natural for us humans to desire (worship) things. To get a sense of how easy we humans desire not just leadership but figureheads, imagine you are observing all that was taking place when Moses was up on Mount Sinai receiving the Ten Commandments. Because Moses had been gone so long, the Jewish people worried that maybe He wasn't returning: "We don't know what has happened to him," they said (Exod. 32:1). Then they said to Aaron (who was put in charge while Moses was away), "Come, make us gods who will go before us."

So Aaron said to the people, "'Then break off your golden earrings from your wives, daughters and sons and bring them to me' . . . and he (Aaron) fashioned the gold into a molded calf, and they rose early on the next day, offered burnt offerings and brought peace offerings" (Exod. 32:2, 4, 6).

When God observed the Israelites making a golden calf, He was furious! "They have turned aside from what I commanded," God said to Moses. "They made an idol and worshiped it and sacrificed to it. . . . My wrath burns hot against them and I may consume them" (Exod. 32:8, 10).

This shows that it's best not to mess with God! This is a good example of what we learned in the previous chapter, where you read that on some level we should "fear" God. God expects us to obey His laws. Again, He has His reasons. It is not that God is simply a jealous tyrant—although He admits to jealousy: "I the Lord am a jealous God." Have you ever wondered what God means by that? As a teen, I wondered why God would be jealous of anything, especially when in this very Commandment He asks us not to be jealous of others nor of the things they have. But God wants us to obey His laws because He wants His children (that's us!) to return to Him. He loves us. He is serious about spelling out what it is we are to do—and not do—that we might know life everlasting. Just as with our parents, there is much love behind the rules. Know the rules. And abide by them. Your life as a Christian is what this earthly journey is about.

To finish our story, Moses, duly afraid for his people, pleaded with God not to be angry. Mercifully (and just as you've probably experienced when your parents threatened to ground you for life—and didn't), God lets them off the hook: "Then the Lord relented and did not bring on His people the disaster He had threatened" (Exod. 32:14). What a loving Father!

What Does God Consider an "Idol"?

It is God's intent, then, that He be first in our minds, our hearts and our lives. *Anything* that crowds out our love for God as our first and primary mission in life is an "idol"—be it a person, money, position or power, and so on. Why would it be important for God to demand such total allegiance? Because when we put other things before our love of God, then it becomes impossible to live a holy life. Complacency, pride, greed, jealousy and fear, for example, keep us alienated from God. Thus, we are no longer "in relationship" with Him. We are no longer acting out His will; we are no longer on the mission of our lives—which is to be worthy of the journey home to God.

Perhaps we feel guiltless because we identify this concept with the Israelites who melted down their gold and created a golden calf. We consider ourselves far wiser than to do something like that! But even if we're not creating golden idols, we have our visual aids, too. It may be a person, such as an evangelist, a minister or youth pastor. As long it enriches our worship of God, this can be useful and valuable. However, the danger is in valuing the object or person too much so that it turns our focus away from God. Sometimes this is a subtle shift, and we may not notice it—unless and until the obvious hits us over the head! Sixteen-year-old Shannon Aldridge tells of an incident in which a "screaming heart" alerted her to this reality.

A year ago I went through a period in my life when every-thing seemed bleak and hopeless. I began searching for a way to fill up what I could only describe as an empty hollow feeling. I knew I needed help, so I got involved in a youth group that met every Thursday evening right after school. The first couple of weeks I attended, I listened and took to heart the mes-sage of the importance of having a personal relationship with Jesus as a means of filling the void. God was my source of com-fort and the reason I attended. By the third week I was even more interested in attending, but my reason for gladly going was a little different. The group leader was a twenty-four-year-old college student, someone I found extremely attractive. I think it would be safe to say I was falling in love. When I first started going, I sat in the very back row. By the third session, I was in the middle row. The fourth time, I was front and center!

Halfway through the sessions, disaster struck. Mike was no longer heading the class. He'd gone off to attend a master's degree program in another state. He was replaced by a female graduate student who was also working toward a master's degree. And there I was, my heart screaming because Mike was no longer there for me!

Two weeks later, I came up with an excuse not to attend the Thursday youth meeting, and this continued the next week, and the next. That's when I realized that while I'd started attending for the right reasons, my later attendance was for the wrong reasons. I wasn't coming to get to know God better. I had been focusing on getting to know Mike better. Without meaning to, I made Mike my idol. If I'm completely honest, I'd have to say that I looked forward to each session because Mike was there. It was all about Mike. Once he was gone, I lost interest in attending youth group.

I'm going back on a regular basis again, and this time my love affair is with God. And yes, the emptiness I was feeling is being filled with a joy that is most welcomed.

—Shannon Aldridge, 16

"Oh God, I Think Thou Hast Outdone Thyself!"—Edna St. Vincent Millay

As we saw with Shannon, something (or someone) can become an idol even without our knowing it—as was also true for sixteen-year-old Nick Hallenbeck, whose "idol" wasn't a person but, rather, nature.

> *I really like to surf. Not so long ago, that's all I wanted to do. When I was riding the waves, I was in heaven! When I wasn't surfing, I was thinking about it, dreaming about it, waxing my board, making plans in my head. It was an all-consuming passion that took total priority over God. Go to church or go to the beach? No-brainer decision there! I was at the beach! I had to admit that I was completely undisciplined, and surfing was way more important to me than it should have been. I still love surfing, but now it doesn't control me. God is on the throne of my life because He's the only One who deserves that position. I don't surf any less, but God doesn't take second to my surfing.*
>
> **—Nick Hallenbeck, 16**

As we see from the remarks by both Shannon and Nick, "idols" can seem innocent enough. Since the beginning of time, people have idolized the forces of nature, even making up various gods to explain what they thought of nature's blessings. We gaze in awe at the majestic mountains, stare in wonderment at the seemingly endless ocean, speculate the height of a stately redwood tree, gawk at the edge of the Grand Canyon because we can hardly believe what our eyes are seeing. Still, nature is not a god. It does not bestow blessings. Yes, we look at God's creative genius in the variety of animals and realize in astonishment that all creation works together to sustain life. Still, it works together because of God. We touch a beautiful flower and are reminded of the words of Jesus who said, "Not even Solomon in all his splendor was dressed like one of these" (Matt. 6:29). Still, the beauty and splendor of a flower is painted by the hand of God.

No doubt about it, creation is more than awesome, and God wants His children to live within and amongst it! But not even the beauty of nature is to supercede our worship of God. The danger comes when we stargaze into nature and lose sight of the one true living God who created it. Perhaps you've heard someone say, "I don't go to church because I can look around and appreciate God in all I see." Yes, God wanted us to look at creation and realize its splendor. But we must know it is not for worship; it could not have come into existence without a genius of colossal proportions orchestrating its formation. That genius is God! Specifically, Jesus Christ! Did you know that Jesus was with the Father at creation and was, indeed, the Creator? "In the beginning was the Word [Jesus], and the Word was with God and the Word was God. He was with God in the beginning. Through him all things were made; without him nothing was made that has been made. . . . The world was made through him. . . . The Word became flesh and lived for a while among us" (John 1:1–3; 10, 14).

God is a Creator worthy of our worship!

What Is Your "Idol of Choice"?

Shannon became so infatuated with her youth leader that her attendance at youth group functions was for all the wrong reasons, rather than because of her desire to learn more about God. Nick allowed his love of surfing to come before his love of Sunday worship.

How about you? Has anything come between you and God? Now that you've had the opportunity to learn more about God's intent behind His second Commandment, take a moment—once again—to think about all the things that would qualify in your life as "idols"—things that overshadow your love for God as being at the core of your life. Review your previous list and revise it if necessary. Are there any additions—idols of choice—on your list? What is more important than the length of the list, of course, is your willingness to have a talk with God about helping you restore Him to His rightful place in your life.

God Is Worthy of Our Worship

There's a story about a man named Thorwaldsen who carved a beautiful statue of Christ. The statue represented Jesus as having his hands outstretched and his head bowed. Someone who saw the statue complained, "I cannot see his face." The sculptor replied, "If you would see the face of Christ, you must get on your knees."

God is God. Let Him be your God. Make Him number one in your life. *To pursue God* is the reason we are given the days we are given. God is the reason. Let us never bow down to another: "I will not give My glory to another" (Isa. 42:8).

YOUR PERSONAL JOURNAL

In what ways does God's second Commandment apply to your life today? In what ways is it still relevant?

_____

_____

_____

_____

_____

Think about your lifestyle. In what ways do you break the second Commandment?

_____

_____

_____

_____

_____

In what ways do you uphold the second Commandment?

_____

_____

_____

_____

_____

In what ways are the first and second Commandments different?

_____

_____

_____

_____

_____

As in all the Commandments, God guards something that is of great importance to our welfare. Why and how is the second Commandment important to *your* welfare?

_____

_____

_____

_____

_____

_____

"Teach me to do your will, for you are my God" (Ps. 143:10a). What does this Scripture mean to you?

_____

_____

_____

_____

_____

"I, the Lord your God, am a jealous God, punishing the children for the sin of the fathers to the third and fourth generation of those who hate Me" (Exod. 20:5). What does this Scripture mean to you? Do you believe things going on in your life (good, bad and neutral) are a product of generations before you? Explain.

_____

_____

_____

_____

_____

_____

Have you ever discussed Exodus 20:5 with your youth pastor, family or friends? Why or why not? Write down any questions you might like to ask them.

- _____
  _____

- _____
  _____

- _____
  _____

- _____
  _____

In what ways do the things you desire and to which you aspire take priority over your time and need for God? What's your plan for setting new priorities? Do you think that the events going on in the world—such as the terrorist attack on September 11, 2001—caused some people to reprioritize the placement of God in their lives? Explain.

_____

_____

_____

_____

_____

Are you "good to go" on the second Commandment, or do you feel you need to have a talk with God? Has anything come between you and God?

_____

_____

_____

_____

_____

God wants to be first in our minds, our hearts and our lives. Why does God demand such total allegiance?

_____

_____

_____

_____

_____

What do you consider to be the purpose of human life on Earth? Do you feel we are all on a mission, and if so, is the mission the same for everyone? In what ways do the friends we choose and the work we do benefit or detract from that mission?

_____

_____

_____

_____

_____

Shannon became so infatuated with her youth leader that her attendance at a youth group was more about seeing Mike, the pastor who led the youth group, than her desire to learn more about God. Has that—or a similar experience—ever happened to you? Explain.

_____

_____

_____

_____

_____

"Oh God, I think Thou hast outdone Thyself!" What do you think the great poet Edna St. Vincent Millay meant by this? What does it mean to you?

_____

_____

_____

_____

_____

We touch a beautiful flower and remember that Jesus said, "Not even Solomon in all his splendor was dressed like one of these" (Matt. 6:29). When was the last time you looked around and felt as Jesus did? To what were you referring—a flower, a beautiful person, a newborn kitty or what?

_____

_____

_____

_____

_____

In the parable about a man named Thorwaldsen (who carved a statue of Christ) someone complained, "I cannot see his face." To this the sculptor replied, "If you would see the face of Christ, you must get on your knees." What do you think he meant by this?

_____

_____

_____

_____

_____

In what ways would the world be different if everyone upheld God's second Commandment?

_____

_____

_____

_____

_____

_____

In what ways would the world be different if *you* upheld God's second Commandment?

_____

_____

_____

_____

_____

_____

How can you keep from growing complacent about upholding God's second Commandment?

_____

_____

_____

_____

_____

_____

THE THIRD
COMMANDMENT

You shall not take [misuse] the name of the Lord Your God in vain, for the Lord will not hold anyone guiltless who takes his name in vain.

Exod. 20:7

As you know, in each Commandment God guards something that is of the greatest importance to our welfare. In the previous chapter you learned how God commanded in His second law that we not worship or serve an idol of any kind. He is to be our One and only. By asking that we place our love for Him above all else, God is safeguarding our opportunity to come to know Him as our Lord and Savior.

In this study of the third Commandment, we learn that God safeguards yet another avenue for our knowing and loving Him: When we say or hear His name, immediately our hearts should joyously identify Him as our Creator, our benevolent Heavenly Father, our Redeemer and Savior. Should we slander or diminish God's name, then our own disrespect will grow, and we may very well lose sight of all that God is to us. Therefore, we are not to dishonor His name in any way—and, we might conclude, we're to ask others to do likewise. We are to uphold His name as sacred and holy—as we profess when we say the Lord's Prayer: "Our Father, which art in heaven, *hallowed* be Thy name." The third Commandment, then, demands that we not misuse God's name, either by swearing, slandering, bearing false witness or deception. This Commandment has other implications as well: We should so love our Heavenly Father so that we call upon Him in times of need and, because we love Him, we should worship Him with praise and thanksgiving.

As always, our Father lets us know there are rewards for honoring this Commandment, and, likewise, consequences when we do not. In this case, the consequence is a part of the Commandment itself: "The Lord will not hold anyone guiltless who takes His name in vain." Upholding the third Commandment shows that we revere, love and trust God, and love each other as God loves each of us.

Is God's Third Commandment Still Relevant Today?

How does this Commandment speak to us in today's times? We live in a world in which taking a young child, a senior citizen or a Christian friend to a movie is often the cause of many uncomfortable moments. Even in PG-rated movies, action heroes and heroines swear (sometimes profusely), frequently taking God's name in vain without so much as wincing or blinking an eye. It makes you feel as though that actor or actress doesn't know God on a personal level, because surely he or she wouldn't curse or speak about the Heavenly Father in this way—and for all the world to hear! Cursing when you've just hit your finger with the hammer is one thing, but taking God's name in vain when on the big screen is quite another. Even some of the most revered among us use profanity as common language, and, in some places, young people aren't considered cool by their peers if they can't spew off cusswords as naturally as they might a smile.

It's a time of not really knowing who is telling the truth. Far too often, you're not wrong until proven wrong—it takes a court, not one's conscience, to convict. Even the gravity of calling upon God to personally observe and witness your "truth-telling" while under oath seems to have lost its supremacy as ultimate fact-finding. For some people, having one's hand upon the Bible—even in a court of law—is simply "standard procedure," and swearing to tell the truth is taken about as seriously as placing their hand upon *A Tale of Two Cities*. For some, it's debatable if having their hand upon the Bible is even a *concept* they understand. Is being wrong okay as long as you can get away with it?

What does the third Commandment mean for you, a seeker of truth living in a time of easy cheating, white lies and outright deception at seemingly every turn? A time in which so many people frequently misrepresent themselves with cool ease—even well-known evangelists have been known to embezzle money under the guise of doing God's work. Is there no end to things being faked, forged or fictitious, to trickery, treachery and time-released truths?

Why Is It So Important to God That We Keep His Name Holy?

Certainly nothing could be more important for our welfare than God's name: "He makes the sun to rise . . . and sends the rain" (Matt. 5:45). Therefore, we must keep *any* and *all* of the titles for which we address God as sacred, including Father, Creator, Jehovah, Redeemer, Jesus or Savior. All show His omnipotence. "God" means "source of all good"; "Jehovah" means "I am that I am." "Jesus," "Savior," "Almighty" and "Christ" mean "the anointed one" or "Messiah."

The name God stands for "His being"—which reveals Him to us. God allows us to know His name because He wants us to have a personal relationship with Him. We are to come to Him daily in prayer. We are to ask Him into our lives so that He will walk with us every day of our lives. He is a promise-making God, one who offers a generation-to-generation blessing, sealed by the gift of redemption. If we want the blessings that follow, we must never misuse His name. And why would we want to? He is our everything.

- God is the giver of life: "The Lord God breathed into his nostrils the breath of life, and the man became a living being" (Gen. 2:7).

- God is the granter of mercy: "Give thanks to the Lord, for He is good; His love endures forever" (Ps. 106:1).
- God is the source of soul-fulfillment: "Let them give thanks to the Lord for His unfailing love and His wonderful deeds for men! For He satisfies the thirsty and fills the hungry soul with good things" (Ps. 107:9).
- God is the wellspring of comfort: "He heals the broken-hearted" (Ps. 147:3); "Come to me, all you who are weary and burdened, and I will give you rest. Take My yoke upon you and learn from Me, for I am gentle and humble in heart, and you will find rest for your souls" (Matt. 11:28).
- God is the source of fellowship: "For where two or three come together in My name, there am I with them" (Matt. 18:20).
- God is the grantor of our prayers: "If you believe, you will receive whatever you ask for in prayer" (Matt. 21:22).
- God grants the desires within our hearts: "Ask and it will be given to you; seek, and you will find; knock, and the door will be opened to you" (Matt. 7:7).
- God is redeemer, giver of salvation and eternal life: "Praise the Lord, O my soul . . . who forgives all your sins and heals all your diseases, who redeems your life from the pit and crowns you with love and compassion, who satisfies your desires with good things" (Ps. 103:2–5).

God's blessings are endless, of course. Yes, God is Holy, and so we should associate His name only with Holiness: "Praise the Lord, O my soul; all my inmost being, praise His holy name" (Ps. 103:1). By holding all that He stands for sacred and revered, we hold onto our opportunity to know Him as our Lord and Savior.

We must never take His name in vain. We need His blessings.

What Does God Consider "Misuse" of His Name?

It is almost unthinkable that we should misuse God's name in any way, be it slandering, bearing false witness or deception or in any other way. Do you? If so, do you do this on purpose, knowing and not caring that by doing so, you are diminishing His reputation in your eyes—and, quite possibly, in the eyes of someone hearing you? Do you do this knowing that God is the omnipotent force behind our reason for existence—as well as Savior, our chance for eternal life? Or do you "take God's name in vain" pretty much because up to now you've been oblivious to all that God is? You're about to read how other young adults strive to uphold God's third Commandment, but before you read their thoughts, consider where you stand on upholding God's third law and write down your thoughts on page 87.

Were you surprised by your response to the ways you misuse God's name? Had you considered that by diminishing God's name, you were also diminishing your desire to come to Him in prayer, praise and thanksgiving? In thinking about what you've been reading in this chapter, does it help you in making the decision to always uphold His third Commandment? It will not be easy, especially if you've been in the habit of swearing and taking His name in vain. And it will be difficult to always practice since many around you may not. You probably will be called a "goody two-shoes" more than once. But hold onto your resolve. The relationship you hold with God is between you and God—and the person who ridicules you has to answer for the ways he or she upholds God's Commandment. And here's another way to think about this: You will be showing leadership for those around you.

Here are three ways we show God that we revere, love and trust Him so as not to transgress against His third Commandment.

Three Ways We Keep God's Name Holy— A Word from Your Peers

1. *We show respect for God's name.* To use God's name without respect is one way we misuse His name. Even using God's name when not calling upon Him in reverence, such as in "Oh God, that test was brutal!" is showing disrespect for God. The following young people show what it means to respect God's name.

> *To me, respecting God's name shows up in the way we turn to God in times of need. I have so much love and respect for God that I don't ever want to misuse His name. I turn to Him all the time—why would I want to alienate Him? Sometimes I need God for little things—like asking for help to get through some particular issue or problem, such as a semester final. And sometimes it's to help me through something really big—like my grandfather's death. Two years ago my grandfather passed away, and I felt so totally sad on some days, even mad. I just loved my grandpa so much; I'd lost a truly best friend. Gramps lived with us for the last few years of his life, and I got to know him and appreciate how much he loved me and supported me in my life. Sometimes I'd come home late from a game or something, and there on my dresser would be a bag of my favorite cookies—with a note congratulating me on our team's win or a positive message if we'd lost. He always called around to get the score. He was just full of love and belief in me. I miss that more than I can put into words.*
>
> *In the first year after he died, I would go where he and I used to walk—and sometimes I'd recall some of the conversations we had, even his goofy jokes. There isn't a day that goes by that I don't wish I still had him in my life. Sometimes, I still go sit on the old back porch—and cry. Do I need God in these times? Yes, I do. Sometimes I ask God to please make sure Gramps*

made it into heaven, and sometimes I just ask God if He'd mind sending Gramps back for a day, even if it was just to sit high up in the bleachers and watch me at baseball practice. And sometimes I just ask God to relieve the pit in my stomach over missing my grandfather as much as I still do. Always, I know that God hears my prayers.

My parents and I are really close, so I can talk to them about anything. But they can't calm and comfort me over my grandpa's death in the same way God can. I take particular comfort in that God was there with my grandfather through the hour of his dying. I saw the power and the comfort in that. So when I say the word "God," it's all about majesty for me. God and I know each other; I wish all my friends had this sort of relationship with God, because it's the source of all that is good, and powerful. I would encourage anyone NOT to use God's name in any way other than with serious thought. I'd say that if you don't love God, if you don't know God, well, that's your great loss. Don't stoop so low as to demean the God I know, the one I turn to all the time.

—Jimmy Van Norman, 20

Personally, I feel we disrespect God's name—take God's name in vain—a lot more than we think we do. As I see it, when Moses asked God for His name, God replied, "I AM." If I AM is the name of God, then whenever we say those words, we are claiming our godhood. But mostly we do it in vain, without power. When I pointed that out once to a good friend, she said, "That's just too much responsibility." I think that's the core of the world's problems—we are afraid to assume the power of being the "heirs" that we are.

Whenever I speak the words "I am" followed by expressions like "tired," "sick," "helpless," and so on, I diminish the name of God. And, by extension, since I create with my thoughts, every thought of powerlessness amounts to abdicating responsibility for cocreating heaven on Earth. So what am I doing about it? I work each day to be a clearer channel for the light to flow through, and I remind myself at every opportunity that I am not this little ego-self, but something infinitely more vast and powerful. All the peace that God is, I am. I am working to live that every moment. I believe it is a responsibility Jesus asks us to shoulder.

—Carol Slater, 22

For me, respecting God's name is spelled out in our display of love for Him. I think it's easy to say "I love God," you know, sort of like parents and kids say to each other, "Love you." Saying this is good, but we tend not to stop and think about the importance of the words we've just let roll off our tongues. I think the real power behind love and respect for God, and for each other, shows up in our actions. So because I love and trust God, I have to ask myself, "How would God know that I really do?" My respect for God has to show up in my actions on a daily basis—and not just in church on Sunday. If I really love God, then I walk with Him daily through prayer. I "talk the walk" and "walk the talk," that sort of thing. I offer thanks for my life, and for the opportunity to be alive yet another day. And I turn to Him for help in all decisions. I go to Him with all my needs—whether I'm feeling hurt, confused or just sad. I talk with Him—for whatever reasons. If I just complain to my friends, teachers or parents but don't take my issues to God, then I'm showing a lack of respect for His power to help me in my life. He can see when I don't love and trust Him enough to hold Him in His rightful place in my life—which is to be number one. I make time for God in my life. I ask Him to be with me and to walk with me always. Respecting God's name—to me—is about respecting God. God and His name are synonymous.

—Karen Willis, 16

For me, respecting God's name is making sure I see the world through the eyes of God. As an example, I trust that while I don't always know why things happen as they do, I realize that God has something in mind that I don't understand. I have a friend who says he's not "religious" because "a real God wouldn't allow people to suffer in any way, either from serious illnesses or starvation, nor would He allow wars." I empathize with my friend's point of view, but I think we have to remember that God is working with the big picture, and all we can see is a little corner of it. Who are we to make assumptions about God's side of the picture? I mean, when He sees suffering, He's got to be sorrowful as well. I don't blame God or see Him as the cause of mankind's problems and suffering. I see God as the source of understanding and comfort. I hope I always remember to ask God to help me understand and trust that He knows best. If and when I do that, I'm showing respect for God—and His name.

—Terrance White, 16

2. *We do not use profanity.* Swearing is another way we break God's third Commandment. "Bless and do not curse," we are told in Romans 12:14. Do you swear? The Bible has much to say on this: "But I tell you, do not swear at all: either by heaven, for it is God's throne, or by the Earth, for it is His footstool; or by Jerusalem, for it is the city of the great King. And do not swear by your head, for you cannot make even one hair white or black. Simply let your 'Yes' be 'Yes' and your 'No,' 'No'; anything beyond this comes from the evil one" (Matt. 5:34–37). Have you thought about why people curse God or swear? Your peers offer these possible explanations:

I think people swear because they fall into the "Hello? Anyone home in there?" category. I know friends who fault God for really dumb things, like feeling He didn't answer a request like, "Please don't let Grandma die," or "Please let so-and-so ask me to the dance," or "Please make sure I get elected to the cheer-leading squad." So to them, their so-called love of God is depen-dent upon God having proven Himself as worthy of love by fulfilling the request. I know others who swear just because they aren't aware that swearing is against God's rules. So I think many young people swear because they're "oblivious."

—Katie Luketic, 17

I think people swear because they're agnostic (a person who does not believe in God). I think there are more agnostics in young adults than we might want to believe. I think it can be a natural time to feel that God is only for senior citizens—as in, "Okay, I'm getting on in years; better be thinking about life after here." But I think a lot of young people don't think of God as a God for all ages. Not many teens know or understand the Commandments, thinking they're an old set of biblical jargon that seem impossible to uphold in today's times, so they fail to even check them out and see how relevant they are to all the things young people face. So, if you are not practicing your faith, if you've walked away from it—even "just for now"—then you're agnostic. And being agnostic, you're less likely to see swearing for what it is: foul, hateful, gross, hard and vengeful—and sinning against the third Commandment.

—Geoff Briars, 15

At my school, a lot of teens swear because it's seen as "cool." They're just following the crowd even if swearing is something they personally don't believe in doing. But I do think some kids swear because they're just mean or angry people. I used to swear a lot when hanging around certain friends. At the time, I considered it a "guy thing." But then I went to church camp and met some really cool guys—and none of them swore. So then I decided that it wasn't so much a "guy thing" as it was just a bad habit my friends had. So from the time I came home from camp, I didn't swear anymore. A year ago, I gave my life to Christ. Not only do I not swear any-more, but now when someone does—especially if they take God's name in vain—I'm really bothered by it.

—Weston Feldman, 16

When my best girlfriends get together, we do swear—and quite a lot. It's sort of a way of relating, like everyone feels equal when we swear. But I've stopped swearing. I realized it wasn't a very cool thing to do, although at the time, I didn't see it as wrong. Like I'd say, "Damn it!" or "Damn you!" or "Oh, damn!" but I never wanted God to damn anyone or anything, so why was I saying it? Then I realized it was because I was "misguided"—that I was swearing without understanding that doing this showed I didn't love God or have respect for God's name. Now I no longer swear, and I find that when someone swears in front of me, I don't like it and I'll say some-thing—especially if they're taking God's name in vain. When I use God's name now, I do it with reverence.

—Cammie Otis, 15

Do you swear? If so, ask God to help you love Him more so that you stop disrespecting Him in this way. Cursing surely dis-pleases our Lord: "Anyone who does these things is detestable to the Lord" (Deut. 18:12). Therefore we should make a conscious decision not to swear. We do this not only because God asks it of us, but because we have a responsibility to those around us: It can cause those around us to lose faith in God's Word.

While profanity has become so commonplace in today's times, something we take for granted, it is still a sin against our Heavenly Father. Can you think of any way in which we use God's name that is acceptable? For example, we carry coins in our pockets that are inscribed "In God We Trust." Is that okay with God?

Although the Word of God forbids swearing, it makes the exception for being sworn in as an officer of the law or as a witness. Christ himself testified under oath when the high priest appealed to Him (Matt. 26:63–64). In fact, one of the saddest moments in the Bible comes when Jesus was put under oath by Caiaphas the high priest who demanded: "I put you under oath by the living God; tell us if you are the Christ, the Son of God!" To this Jesus replied, "Yes, it is as you say . . . But, I say to all of you, in the future you will see the Son of Man sitting at the right hand of the Mighty One, and coming on the clouds of heaven" (Matt. 26:64). This response simply exasperated the priest, who the Bible says "tore at his clothing" and pronounced all as "blasphemy." You probably know the rest of the story (and if not, be sure to read the book of Matthew); all leads directly to the court saying, "He [Jesus] is worthy of death" (Matt. 26:66).

Have you ever been put under oath? It's serious business. As Peter Johnson, seventeen, explains:

> *My dad was called as a witness in a court case involving a liquor store robbery. Before he went to court to testify, he was like, "I'll bet it was the guy in the black sweatshirt. I'm making sure somebody pays [for what he did]." The truth is, my dad wasn't really sure who all was involved in the crime because there were six total in the store when he was there. Things happened so fast that my dad wasn't all that sure of who did what. But one guy, in his words, "looked like he'd be the guy to do such a thing."*
>
> *Then, after Dad took the stand, he was asked to take the oath. Well, that clarified his thinking. At that point, my dad realized he was to tell what he knew, not just to the judge and attorneys and others within the courtroom, but that God had been called in as well. That's when he realized just how big a responsibility he had to tell the truth—that he had not witnessed the robbery firsthand and he'd have to put his*

prejudices aside. As my dad told me, "There I was, my hand upon the Bible, and I realized I was promising, with God as my witness, to tell the 'whole truth and nothing but the truth.'"

Bringing God into the picture was a serious thing to him—as it should be. All this has made me think about the reality of calling on God's name. It's to be taken very seriously.

—Peter Johnson, 17

Peter makes an important point, one that thirteen-year-old Lannie Glick found out when a girl didn't believe something she'd told her, and so she asked, "Do you swear on a stack of Bibles?" As Lannie commented, "When we want the ultimate truth, we refer to God as the ultimate 'you'd-better-or-else' proof to make sure we're getting it."

3. *We do not pervert God's Word.* Perverting God's Word is another way we misuse His name. To "pervert" means to misrepresent. Throughout the Bible, God has much to say about this, especially in the book of Leviticus (19:11–18 NKJV): "You shall not steal, nor deal falsely, nor lie to one another. And you shall not swear by My name falsely, nor shall you profane the name of your God; I am the Lord. You shall not cheat your neighbor nor rob him. You shall not curse the deaf, nor put a stumbling block before the blind; I am the Lord. You shall do no injustice in judgment. You shall not be partial to the poor, nor honor the person of the mighty. In righteousness you shall judge your neighbor. You shall not go about as a talebearer among your people; . . . I am the Lord. You shall not hate your brother in your heart. . . . You shall not take vengeance, nor bear any grudge against the children of your people, but you shall love your neighbor as yourself: I am the Lord."

How do we "pervert" God's Word? We misrepresent God when we "deceive by His name" or are hypocritical. People often do not recognize their own hypocrisy; they don't see how they are saying one thing and living another. For example, if we say we are Christians, but fail to abide by God's Commandments, then we are perverting the Word of God. "These people honor Me with their lips; but their hearts are far from Me" (Matt. 15:8).

The following teens put this in context.

When someone tells me he or she is a Christian and then that person puts me down or makes a really cutting remark, I instantly discount that person as being a Christian. This happens a lot at my school. Maybe it's because it's a Christian school, so there is this perception that we're somehow all Christians, which isn't the case, in my opinion. Some kids just go to my school because it has a reputation for having good teachers and because the classes are small. But that doesn't mean everyone who enrolls is necessarily a Christian. Still, we kids tend to judge everyone by "Christian" standards. I know how easy it is to be "godly" while I'm in church, but on Monday, I'm back to my old ways. I'm making a point of not being a Jekyll and Hyde, of having two sides to me. I am a Christian, so I try to always remember to ask myself, "What would Jesus do?" and then do that.

—Bruce Walkins, 17

The way I see this hypocrisy playing out is that sometimes when I bow my head to pray in the cafeteria, some dude will come up and whap me on the head while I'm praying. Obviously, that's an intentional way of saying, "Oh look, Bruce is a Jesus Freak." So I'm somehow supposed to feel bad about asking God to bless my food, but when my grandmother died, this same kid said, "Sorry to hear about your grandma. My prayers are with you." Well, I don't think so! If your prayers are with me because I lost my grandma, then let your prayers be with me as I ask God to bless the food I eat. God is not a fair-weather friend. God is for all times. So we should all see Him for all times.

—Buddy Moreno, 14

Keeping God's Name Holy

Using God's name in disrespectful ways can drive God out of your life. It happens all around us and is an easy habit to get into, but that's all the more reason to be vigilant, to watch your thoughts and words to make sure you are honoring God. Another reason it is so important to watch our own behavior is so as not to stop our own Christian growth. As twenty-five-year-old police officer, Douglas Marx, says: "I am still growing in the Lord, and He continues to use me every day for His good purpose. I am very excited to see what He has in store for me. Lately I have overcome some pretty major hurdles in my personal walk, and by doing so, only because of Him, I see things more clearly than I ever have before. I pray that I keep this perspective and remember my place in creation. Every day I ask God to bless me—and all of us—that He might provide us with all that is necessary to carry out his perfect will."

We all have great need of God. Ours is a Father in heaven with whom we can call upon to walk with us every step of the way. Let us keep His name Holy; let us call out His name with the utmost reverence and respect.

YOUR PERSONAL JOURNAL

In what ways does God's third Commandment apply to your life today? In what ways is it still relevant?

_____

_____

_____

_____

_____

_____

Think about your lifestyle. In what ways do you break the third Commandment?

_____

_____

_____

_____

_____

_____

In what ways do you uphold the third Commandment?

_____

_____

_____

_____

_____

_____

Why is it so important to God that you keep His name holy?

_____

_____

_____

_____

_____

_____

Does God say that we should not use His name at all? Explain.

_____

_____

_____

_____

_____

_____

Swearing is one way we misuse God's name. Why do you think people curse? Do your friends swear? Why or why not?

_____

_____

_____

_____

_____

_____

Do you swear? Why? How do you feel about swearing?

_____

_____

_____

_____

_____

_____

If you do swear, in what ways has this chapter influenced you to break this habit? How do you intend to stop swearing—will you ask God to make swearing against your nature; or ask your parents or friends to call you on it each time you do?

_____

_____

_____

_____

_____

_____

If you have family or friends who swear, how might you influence them to give up swearing?

_____

_____

_____

_____

_____

_____

_____

Scripture says, "Anyone who does these things is detestable to the Lord" (Deut. 18:12). What does this Scripture verse mean to you?

_____

_____

_____

_____

_____

In what ways do you feel that swearing can cause those around you to lose faith in God or God's Word? Explain.

_____

_____

_____

_____

_____

What can you do if one of your friends repeatedly swears? Have you ever told someone that his or her swearing was offensive to you? If yes, what did the other person say in response to you?

_____

_____

_____

_____

_____

Bearing false witness is another way we misuse God's name. Give an example of a time when you did this. Did you consider your action a sin against God? Explain.

_____

_____

_____

_____

_____

_____

This third Commandment indicates that because we love our Heavenly Father, we should worship Him with prayer, praise and thanksgiving. How do you see this as "respecting" God's name?

_____

_____

_____

_____

_____

God wants us to keep *any* and *all* of the titles for which we address God as sacred, be it Father, Creator, Jehovah, Redeemer, Jesus, Savior, Almighty or Christ. How do you feel when you hear any of these names taken in vain? What do you do about it?

_____

_____

_____

_____

_____

Carol Slater said that whenever she speaks the words "I am" followed by expressions like "tired," "sick," "helpless," and so on, she takes the name of God in vain. What do you think about this?

_____

_____

_____

_____

_____

_____

We carry coins in our pockets that are inscribed, "In God We Trust." Is that okay with God, or would He rather we find a different inscription? Why do you think we put "In God We Trust"? Why not, "Have a nice day" or "spend wisely" or some other positive saying?

_____

_____

_____

_____

_____

_____

Although the Word of God forbids swearing, it makes the exception for being sworn in as an officer of the law or as a witness. Why is this so?

_____

_____

_____

_____

_____

_____

What would you do if you were put in a situation in which you were expected to not tell the truth, even while being under oath? What if, in your mind, lying under oath was necessary, for example, to keep your friend or family member from a drastic consequence, such as being fined or going to jail?

_____

_____

_____

_____

_____

_____

Have you ever been asked to place your hand upon the Bible in order that someone might know you were telling the truth? What was the reason for your being under oath? Did you feel nervous, or did the fact that you were "sworn to tell the truth, the whole truth, and nothing but the truth" make you feel you had to tell the entire truth—and that felt good because you could "clear the air" or "get things off your chest" or "level with God"? Explain.

_____

_____

_____

_____

_____

_____

Perverting God's Word is another way we misuse His name. What does this mean to you? Have you ever misused God's name in this way? Explain.

_____

_____

_____

_____

_____

_____

We "pervert" God's word when we "deceive by His name" or are hypocritical. People often don't see how they are saying one thing and living another. What would you do if you noticed your friend behave in this way? Would you confront him or her? What would you do or say?

_____

_____

_____

_____

_____

_____

Using God's name in disrespectful ways can drive Him out of our lives. Do you think it can also cause others to lose their faith—or to not feel a need to accept God as their Savior? Explain.

_____

_____

_____

_____

_____

_____

In what ways would the world be different if everyone upheld God's third Commandment?

_____

_____

_____

_____

_____

_____

In what ways would the world be different if *you* upheld God's third Commandment?

_____

_____

_____

_____

_____

_____

How can you keep from growing complacent about upholding God's third Commandment?

_____

_____

_____

_____

_____

Starving Child

Oh most gracious and loving God,
I sometimes wonder how You speak to us,
And how You get through to Your free-willed children.
I ask: Are You in the rib cage of a starving child,
. . . or the scream of an ambulance in the night,
. . . or the piercing sound of a hostile bullet?
Are You calling out in the shattering of an explosion,
. . . or when an angry knife stops a pulse,
. . . or a cruel word pierces a fragile heart?
Oh, most gracious and comforting God,
Are You saddened when Your children go astray,
. . . when a drunken parent hits a child,
. . . when a best friend dies of leukemia?
Do You grieve when Your children mess up their lives,
. . . too busy to come to You in prayer
. . . too full of ourselves to be grateful?
Oh most gracious and forgiving God,
Thank You for loving and forgiving us
. . . when we think we can mend our own hearts
. . . and work our own miracles.
Oh most gracious and redeeming God,
Teach us to make our will Your own,
. . . how to care for our brothers and sisters
. . . and to tend to our own souls.
Oh most gracious Father and Creator,
Thank You for the evidence of Your abundant love,
. . . in the rising of the sun
. . . in the budding of a flower, and
. . . in the reassuring smile of a friend.
Every day You are right here beside us, and I know it.
Promising a new day and a fresh beginning.
Thank You most gracious and loving God.

—Kimberly Holcombe, 17

READER/CUSTOMER CARE SURVEY

We care about your opinions. Please take a moment to fill out this Reader Survey card and mail it back to us. As a special "thank you" we'll send you exciting news about interesting books and a valuable **Gift Certificate.**

Please PRINT using ALL CAPS

First Name [ ] MI. [ ] Last Name [ ]

Address [ ]

City [ ] ST [ ] Zip [ ]

Phone # ([ ]) [ ] — [ ]   Fax # ([ ]) [ ] — [ ]

Email [ ]

(1) Gender:
___ Female   ___ Male

(2) Age:
___ 12 or under   ___ 40-59
___ 13-19   ___ 60+
___ 20-39

(3) Marital Status
___ Married
___ Single
___ Divorced/Widowed

(4) Did you receive this book as a gift?
___ Yes   ___ No

(6) How did you find out about this book?
Please fill in ONE.
1) ___ Recommendation
2) ___ Store Display
3) ___ Bestseller List
4) ___ Online
5) ___ Advertisement
6) ___ Catalog/Mailing
7) ___ Interview/Review (TV, Radio, Print)

(7) Where do you usually buy books?
Please fill in your top TWO choices.
1) ___ General Bookstore
2) ___ Christian Bookstore
3) ___ Online
4) ___ Book Club/Mail Order
5) ___ Price Club (Costco, Sam's Club, etc.)
6) ___ Retail Store (Target, Wal-Mart, etc.)

(9) What subjects do you enjoy reading about most? Rank only **FIVE.** *Use 1 for your favorite, 2 for second favorite, etc.*

	1	2	3	4	5
1) Parenting/Family	○	○	○	○	○
2) Relationships	○	○	○	○	○
3) Recovery/Addictions	○	○	○	○	○
4) Health/Nutrition	○	○	○	○	○
5) Christian Living	○	○	○	○	○
6) Inspiration	○	○	○	○	○
7) Business Self-Help	○	○	○	○	○
8) Teen Issues	○	○	○	○	○
9) Sports	○	○	○	○	○

(14) What attracts you most to a book?
(Please rank 1-4 in order of preference.)

	1	2	3	4
1) Title	○	○	○	○
2) Cover Design	○	○	○	○
3) Author	○	○	○	○
4) Content	○	○	○	○

TAPE IN MIDDLE; DO NOT STAPLE

BUSINESS REPLY MAIL
FIRST-CLASS MAIL PERMIT NO 45 DEERFIELD BEACH, FL

POSTAGE WILL BE PAID BY ADDRESSEE

FAITH COMMUNICATIONS
3201 SW 15TH STREET
DEERFIELD BEACH FL 33442-9875

FOLD HERE

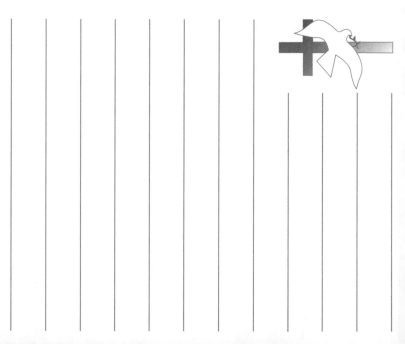

Comments:

THE FOURTH
COMMANDMENT

Remember the Sabbath day by keeping it holy. . . .

Exod. 20:8

I n the last chapter you learned it was of supreme importance to God that we not misuse His name; we are to guard it and keep it holy. We do this to preserve our own sense of God as omnipotent, and because upholding God's third Commandment shows our reverence, love and trust in our Heavenly Father. In this chapter, the study of God's fourth law, we learn that God once again asks us to "guard and keep holy" something. This time, it's the Sabbath, or Sunday.

Sabbath means *rest*. Saturday, the seventh day of the week, was the day of rest in the Old Testament. God gave the Sabbath to Israel for two purposes: First, as a day of rest: "There are six days when you may work, but the seventh day is a Sabbath of rest" (Lev. 23:3), and second, as a day of (public) worship, a time to hear and learn God's Word: "Six days you shall labor and do all your work, but the seventh day is a Sabbath to the Lord your God" (Exod. 20:9–10). The Sabbath, then, is a day to "tend to the needs of body and soul."

The Sabbath always has been a holy day for God. For those using the Roman calendar (most countries), it was on a Sunday that Christ arose from the dead (Easter Sunday). It was on a Sunday that the Holy Spirit was "poured out" and the church was born (Pentecost Sunday). But just as God lets us know that Sunday is the "Lord's Day," He also tells us it is *our* day: "For the Son of Man is Lord of the Sabbath" (Matt. 12:8). After letting us know that this day is a "gift" to us, we're instructed on how we're to use it: to rest and restore ourselves; and to worship and spend time (fellowship) with others.

As with all the other laws, we're to uphold this one. In Exodus 31:13 we hear, "You must observe My Sabbaths. This will be a sign between Me and you for the generations to come, so you may know that I am the Lord who makes you holy." And in

Exodus 31:14, we learn that the misuse of it grieves God: "Observe the Sabbath, because it is holy to you. Anyone who desecrates it must be cut off from his people." Upholding the fourth Commandment shows that we revere, love and trust God, and love our "neighbors" as God loves us.

Is God's Fourth Commandment Still Relevant Today?

Again, in each Commandment God guards something that is of the greatest importance to our welfare. It's not so difficult to see why God's law was so needed over 4,000 years ago—a time of arduous and strenuous work and toil. After all, this was a time in which the demands of daily work were all-consuming, and worship was not just a ten- to twenty-minute automobile ride away. It was a time in which getting together with friends and relatives was perhaps a long journey, not just a matter of dialing them up, hopping on a plane or e-mailing the latest family photos. Surely a day set aside for rest and worship was both a gift and a relief in times of old.

But that was then, and this is now. What possible reasons do we have to take a day of rest? "Slave labor" has been all but abolished, and laws prescribe the length of a typical workday (eight hours). Hands-on laborers now have the convenience of tractors and other related tools to assist them. In fact, doctors and other health experts tell us that we need more—not less—physical activity (which is, presumably, why we've invented workout centers). But are we serious about wanting to lighten our load?

We live in a time of not only the "one-minute manager," but the "one-minute" everything. So who has the time to take a break anyway? Certainly, few of us do, even if it is Sunday. It's nearly impossible these days to discern how Sunday is any different from Monday—or Tuesday or Wednesday or any other day of the week, for that matter. From buying a new pair of sneakers to taking your computer in to be repaired, from apply-ing for a job to working an eight-hour shift, for many, Sunday has the feel of just another workday. Who has time to relax? Besides, if we feel we're facing burnout, there's always a guru who is more than happy to charge us for his time in telling us how to "balance" life. Some may put on good music, but far too many, we learn, resort to drugs in a desperate attempt to escape reality or to "chill out." Do we, with so many conveniences to make life "easier"—only to find out that it is anything but—need to learn the importance of restoring ourselves?

As for worship, well, everyone knows that most young people, given a choice, would rather have a wisdom tooth pulled than go to church. Besides, with all that we've been told about the impor-tance of self-esteem, we're well into the practice of blowing our-selves a kiss in the mirror every morning and saying, "You're special! You're wonderful! You can do it! Go get 'em!" So if we can make ourselves feel good, why do we need the church to help us do it? Besides, we can turn on the radio or television and read-ily see a worship service broadcast from anywhere in the world. And fellowship—isn't that what friends are for?

Does the fourth Commandment still speak to us today? Can it help us learn to restore ourselves in ways that are meaningful to the self, to the soul and to the "neighbors" with whom we are making this earthly journey? What is the application of the fourth Commandment in today's hectic, stress-filled and "multi-tasking" times? Let's take a look.

Is It a Sin to Work on Sunday (and Is Homework Considered Work)?

As you read at the beginning of this chapter, God expects us NOT to work on Sunday: "Six days you shall labor and do all your work, but the seventh day is a Sabbath to the Lord your

God" (Exod. 20:9–10). Now that we're certain it is a sin to "labor" on Sunday, the question is, What does God mean by "work"? Are doing your homework, cleaning your room, doing chores or helping a friend fix up his new apartment considered "work"? What about shopping for groceries, going to your part-time job or taking a babysitting job down the street?

How does God define "work," anyway? We know in some cases that God healed the sick on Sunday, or, as we learn in Matthew 12:8, Jesus went through the grain fields on the Sabbath when his disciples were hungry. And in Matthew 12:10–12, we learn that when he saw a man with a shriveled hand and healed him, Jesus was himself asked, "Is it lawful to heal on the Sabbath?" To this he replied, "If any of you has a sheep and it falls into a pit on the Sabbath, will you not take hold of it and lift it out? How much more valuable is a man than a sheep! Therefore it is lawful to do good on the Sabbath." Does this mean, then, that it is okay to work on the Sabbath under "special circumstances"—for example, when a plumber or doctor responds to an emergency call for his or her services? These are interesting questions—ones you'll want to pose to your parents, teachers, friends and youth minister. Turn to pages 116–17 and make a list of all the questions you might have about observing the Sabbath.

What did you discover in making your list of questions? Did your questions mostly have to do with you, or with your parents or friends? Did they have to do with society at large—such as when did practically every business decide to stay open seven days a week? Did your list raise a lot of questions? For example, are you wondering if it's wrong for a retail business or a restaurant to open their door for business on Sunday, or if working on Sunday implies the business owner is not a "practicing Christian"? Do you ponder such questions? Likewise, do you wonder how God's law is a ready source of rest and renewal— and how incredibly important it is to the times in which we live?

Here are three ways we uphold our Heavenly Father's fourth

Commandment, and what some of your peers have to say about the challenges they face, as well as how living the Commandment in its truest form helps them restore themselves—mind, body and spirit.

Sunday: A Day to Rest and Restore Ourselves

As you recall from chapter 1, the Commandments are the basis for moral and spiritual conduct, as well as the foundation of peace and prosperity for the individual. Setting aside Sunday as a day to rest and sing praises to God was a practice that started during the time of the apostles, as we can see in Acts 20:7 and 1 Corinthians 16:2, as well as Revelation 1:10. Although steeped in the history of biblical times, this Commandment definitely has application for today's times. What could be more important in these uncertain times of fast-paced schedules filled with stress and duress than that we observe Sunday as a day to rest, relax and restore ourselves?

Sunday is a hallowed day. "The Lord blessed the Sabbath day and made it holy" (Exod. 20:11). Using it as it was intended brings many opportunities and blessings. Still, as you look around the "real world" and see so many people working away on Sundays, are you wondering if we've forgotten (or are denying) the fourth Commandment? Natalie Brown, sixteen, discovered the importance of using Sunday in the way God intended.

> I can really understand how easy it is for teens with a life like mine to get sick! My life was once so crazy. There was always so much to get done all the time that I found myself always "beat"—just really dead tired. Sunday was just another day, one that was as busy as the rest, even though I wasn't at school. As a result, when Monday morning rolled around, I was still tired.

All week long I have to get up at 6:30 to get ready for school, and on Saturdays I have to be at work by eight o'clock. So Sunday was the only day I had to get the tons of homework done that I never seem to get done during the week. My days were always so jammed full of activities. My life was so hectic that I was always tired and out of control. I guess my parents thought so, too, because after just two months of my having a part-time job, they told me I could no longer work the Sunday shift and that I had to start attending church with them again.

So now on Sundays I get to sleep in. Then I get up and go to the eleven o'clock Sunday service. This change in my schedule (my mother calls it a "re-ordering of priorities") has been good. Sleeping in at least one day a week feels like a luxury and gives me a chance to rest up. And it feels good to be back at church, too. Once I get there, a sense of peace and tranquility takes over, and I just go with the flow.

Judging by how tired and harried I felt before my "re-ordering of priorities," I think God was telling me I needed "time out." So now I'm taking this time to do just that: Sunday is now a day I look forward to. I get to sleep in; I go to church with my family; and then, once I'm home from church, I eat something, go to my room, put on music I enjoy, and sometimes, take a nap. Then, feeling refreshed, I finish up any homework or start a new project. Sometimes I even have a friend over, or whatever. Now when Monday comes, I feel as though I've had a mini—and much needed—vacation. I'm a real fan of God's fourth Commandment!

—Natalie Brown, 16

Sunday: A Day for Public Worship

Upholding God's fourth Commandment means that we also observe Sunday as a day of worship. While we should glorify the Lord every day of the week—by coming to Him daily in prayer and studying His Word in daily devotions—God asks that we use Sundays specifically to come together for *public* worship. Why? Why can't we just devote time on Sunday to reading and studying God's Word? Can't sitting in front of our TVs, watching a televised church service, suffice? Why is God so specific about "public" worship?

Church: a spiritual family

The answer is that God wants us to view the church as a "spiritual family." Just as in your own family, each person is "looked out for" in a church family. First of all, membership in a church gives you identity. Attending church means we are likely to come to know each other. This is what God wants, even expects of us. God tells us that He considers it the duty of a Christian to pray for the church as a "holy institution," and to pray for the spiritual well-being of all its members, including its pastors, teachers and others who further the Word of God on behalf of the church. We are expected to support the church and its goals—such as provide Sunday school to the young and bring the Word of God to every member who belongs to our congregation. We are to carry the Word of God to other members of the congregation who cannot be in attendance, either because they are ill, infirmed, incarcerated or whatever else keeps them from hearing the Word of God. And yes, maybe just because they've become complacent, "too busy" or lost hope.

We are to tend even to those members who are in attendance. Some need us for encouragement to stay attached to the church while in the throes of their own challenging times. Others need someone to help lift a burden from their shoulders. Whether it is through our charitable contribution or by praying for them, we are to support the members of our spiritual family in their Christian walk—both in spirit and in person.

Does this mean that if we don't belong to a church that we are relieved of helping others to love and trust in God? No. Because we recognize God as the source and center of life, we gather in His name to help and support each other in our spiritual lives. This is the importance of membership in a group that shares your faith, and of coming together for public worship. Some people believe they needn't go to church, temple or a holy place to pay tribute to God. They believe that God hears them no matter where they are, and that is good enough. This interpretation misses the point of why God asks us to come together *publicly*. Publicly we come to the "throne of grace" in petition, in praise, in confession and intercession. "Let us go to the house of the Lord" (Ps. 122:1). Side by side with others, shoulder to shoulder, we acknowledge that He is worthy of our praises sung together: "There is no one holy like the Lord, there is no one besides You. There is no rock like our God" (1 Sam. 2:2).

We're to attend gladly and, yes, stay awake while there

God delights in seeing us come together in His name. And by the way, He expects us to come willingly, even "gladly." And yes, once there, He expects us to stay awake, unlike Eutychus, who when Paul was giving a sermon, nodded off to sleep and fell out of the window, hitting his head so hard they thought the sleepyhead had killed himself! "Seated in a window was a young man named Eutychus, who was sinking into a deep sleep as Paul talked on and on. When he was sound asleep, he fell to the ground from the third story and was picked up dead" (Acts 20:9). (Later they discovered he hadn't died—but it's doubtful Eutychus ever fell asleep during a sermon again!)

God is pleased when He sees His people worship Him. Where God's Word is being preached, then good and truth and light are being shared. Reading the Scriptures and studying God's Word help us to better know God. We misuse Sunday when we make light of the preaching of God's Word or stay away from church services for a poor excuse, or for no reason at all.

How about you? Do your Sunday plans include worshiping your Heavenly Father? If not, it's never too late to begin. How about this coming Sunday? Here's a persuasive testimony from seventeen-year-old Rex O'Connor.

I always used to go to church with my mom and dad. But as a teen, I refused to go. So they let me do my own thing. That was when I was thirteen. When I was fourteen, I got into drugs in a serious way, and it really destroyed my life. It took way over a year of being in an in-house drug rehab program and aftercare to turn myself around. But what really turned my life around was finding God. Just because I went to church when I was younger didn't mean that I knew God.

In the drug rehab center I learned that I was powerless over drugs, and that the only way to get a grip on things was to turn things over to God. By that time, I didn't doubt that it was true; I'd tried everything else to stop using, and nothing worked. Finally, I just asked God to help me, and I promised my life to Him if He'd help me save mine. So now I walk with God, and it's made all the difference in my life. Because I'm a Christian, I attend church every Sunday, no exceptions. I love going. I love the support I get from other Christians. My church has a youth group, and it's great. We talk about God in real life, all the ways we can stay on a path of living decently, and how we can stay true to the Word of God.

Accepting God into my life is the reason I've stayed sober and drug-free. While I talk to God on a daily basis, it's going to church on Sunday that gives me the support base to keep going—which is why I'm now taking my little brother. He's only ten, and already he's smoking cigarettes. So in the last six months, I've made a point of taking him (or the way he puts it, "dragging him along") with me to church. At first he rebelled against going. A couple of times I had to pour a glass of water on his head to get him out of bed. But I did it because I know how important it is that he attend on a regular basis. First, I think it's very important that he see other kids his age going to church. And by attending regularly, he'll get in the habit of going and so he'll have a better chance of making friends who can support him in coming to know and love God.

So now when I say, "Up and out, bro. Time to get ready for church," he knows better than to say "no." I'm going to stay close and encourage him all the way. I'm hoping that going to church is one more step in the right direction of saving him from the heartbreak I caused myself by becoming chemically dependent. I'm hoping his love of God will help him stay clean and sober.

I can see that his going to church is having a good effect on him. After church he's in a good mood and acts like a real buddy. He wants to shoot hoops and just hang out with me. So I try to spend as much time with him as I can because I think that's important. I see him changing little by little. I can see that he's dropping his "tough kid" act: he no longer smokes cigarettes, and he's open to talking about things. I'm giving him the "no drugs" lectures, of course, but just spending time together helps. After we shoot hoops, we watch a little television and then get something to eat. Then I tell him to get out his homework, and he sits at the kitchen table with me while I do mine. None of this happens during the other six days of the week. I'm grateful for Sunday and for the opportunity that setting aside this day brings. Like I said, I'm hoping that my example of brotherly love and then introducing him to God's love will be what it takes for my little brother to do well and not become an addict. Like me, I can see that he finds the Word of God uplifting. Little by little, I can see the effect of God working in his life.

—Rex O'Connor, 17

Sunday: A Day for Fellowship

We observe Sunday as a day of fellowship with others. God's fourth law asks that in addition to making Sunday a day away from work and a time of public worship, we use it as a time to *gather together.* Certainly you could see how Natalie and Rex, by observing Sunday as a day to rest and worship, achieved a natural built-in fellowship with others. This is good, and as it should be.

God wants us to use Sunday as a time to honor Him by celebrating the ties that hold our families and our communities together. He's even promised to "be there" among us: "For where two or three come together in My name, there am I with them" (Matt. 18:20).

In addition to benefiting from setting aside a specific day for rest, recuperation, and social and celebratory time with family and friends, we're to make time to bring the Word of God—which can sometimes take the form of simply bringing our own happy heart and godly spirit—to someone who needs it. This would include making time on Sundays for visiting the sick, shut-ins and others who are in need of spiritual nourishment. We are to use this day to visit those whose spirits need fresh air, such as people in hospitals or the elderly in nursing homes. "Religion that God our Father accepts as pure and faultless is this: to look after orphans and widows in their distress, and to keep oneself from being polluted by the world" (James 1:27).

How do you honor God in this way? Who in your community can benefit from your own happy heart, from all that you have to share? Take a moment to think about this now and, turning to the journal section (pages 118–19), write down ways in which you can do this.

Being needed is such a positive thing, isn't it? Was your list a long one, or did you have a difficult time coming up with ways you can serve your church community? Eleven-year-old Mary Gellens does this by taking her dog to the local children's cancer ward for the kids to pet and play with every other Sunday. Doing this helps take the children's minds off the painful chemotherapy treatments. There are so many ways that you are needed, too. Find something you can share, and then do it! It is sure to change your life, or at the least, have a positive effect on the person you're helping, something that sixteen-year-old Sara Tobias discovered.

> *I'm dating a guy from school who is a Christian. One of the ways he and I spend time together is by my going with him and his family to church on Sunday mornings. After that we go to his house for a big Sunday meal. It's their family ritual— this big meal where family and friends come together. There's something else they do that I find incredibly wonderful: Every Sunday, on the way to church, they stop at a senior-citizen's home and take one to two people to church, always inviting that person or two home with them after services to share the meal. My boyfriend's grandparents from his mother's side of the family come over, and sometimes his uncle and his wife and their two kids come over.*
>
> *I love time at their house because the meal is never rushed, and everyone uses this time to catch up on news about various family members, from the little tots in the family to some of the more senior members. Even the seniors from the nursing home share things—they especially like to talk about their own children and to reminisce about their parents or grandparents— and you should see the joy in their faces when they do! It's just*

a wonderful time; everyone is happy. I love that in my boyfriend's family everyone is checking in on everyone and looking out for them. When my boyfriend's father says grace at the meal, I just know that God is looking in, and He must be very pleased with them.

My family isn't like this at all. I live with my mom; my dad is remarried and lives in another state. I don't have any brothers or sisters, so there is no gathering together, ever. And so far as I know, no one goes to church. My mother doesn't, so I don't—or at least until I started dating my boyfriend. So just about everything I've learned about the fourth Commandment I've learned by being with my boyfriend on Sunday.

I'm hoping my mom will start going to church. She never went to church as a child, so it's not something that is a part of her life—or at least up till now. But I'm hoping she will start. I can see her warming up to the idea, because when I get back on Sunday afternoons, she is always there, and we talk about things. Before, when I'd come in she'd say, "Hi! Did you have fun?" and I'd say, "Yes, thanks for asking," and head to my room. That was pretty much the extent of our talking. Now, because I really want her to go to church so she has the opportunity to hear God's Word and to be with others who can help her feel welcome, I make a point of stopping to talk with her before I start homework and get organized for my school week. Mostly during the week, I'm so busy and tired, so we don't really talk things over, but the time I first get back from being at my boyfriend's house is very different. The time Mom and I spend together then is so positive and loving that we both look forward to it. I think it's because I'm in a "good space" and that contributes to the both of us being in a "good space." I'm hoping all this will help her decide to join a church.

I know that when I get married and have a family, I'm going to do Sundays the same way my boyfriend's family does. There's something very special about coming together with others, praying together and just enjoying each other's company. I like the loving and incredibly peaceful yet empowering energy it creates. I enjoy spending Sunday with this family, and I always love God more when I leave.

—Sara Tobias, 16

Preserving the Gift of a Day Set Aside

God wants us to not permit anything to rob us—and Him—of the blessings of the day of rest, worship and fellowship. "Let us consider how we may spur one another on toward love and good deeds. Let us not give up meeting together, as some are in the habit of doing" (Heb. 10:24–25). How do you keep Sunday as holy as God wants? Do you allow the demands of life to divert your attention from rest, recuperation and service to God's Sundays? If so, what can you do to make it different? Begin by setting goals for the way your Sunday is to be organized. Make a commitment to keep Sunday as a day set apart for the purpose of rest, worship and fellowship. Start Sundays off by attending church. If you don't belong to a church, join one. What faith are you? If you're not sure what church to join, begin your search by asking friends if you can attend church or youth group with them. Ask your counselor at school what youth groups many of the students at your school belong to. Get involved with youth organizations—such as a YWCA or YMCA. There are many ways to find a way to worship God.

What are your plans to be in "fellowship"—to socialize with your friends, and to help and assist those who need spiritual renewal? Think about it and make a goal. Whether this is a phone call to a grandparent—a call in which you are leisurely listening to your grandmother or grandfather and aren't watching the clock, or a visitation to someone in the hospital—do it. Don't lose the opportunity to enrich your life—and that of another—in the way God planned. This is the purpose of the Sabbath. Honor it: This is how you say thank you to our Heavenly Father for giving us His gift of rest for the "body, mind and soul." We are so blessed!

YOUR PERSONAL JOURNAL

In what ways does God's fourth Commandment apply to your life today? In what ways is it still relevant?

_____

_____

_____

_____

_____

_____

Think about your lifestyle. In what ways do you break the fourth Commandment?

_____

_____

_____

_____

_____

In what ways do you uphold God's fourth Commandment?

_____

_____

_____

_____

_____

_____

How is your life improved when you set Sunday apart as a day of rest and relaxation, a time to worship and an opportunity to interact with the members of your congregation and others?

_____

_____

_____

_____

_____

_____

The Lord sets aside a separate day for worship, but are not all days holy? Explain.

_____

_____

_____

_____

_____

_____

In what ways do you use Sundays to restore yourself? If you don't currently do this, what can you do, and how would doing so be beneficial to your life?

_____

_____

_____

_____

_____

_____

_____

Do you attend church regularly? Why? In what ways is attending beneficial to your life?

_____

_____

_____

_____

_____

_____

_____

Where do you go to church? Are you a member, or do you just drop in? Why? In what ways do you feel that being a member of a congregation adds to your willingness to get involved in the church "community"—such as food drives and attending youth camp?

_____

_____

_____

_____

_____

_____

_____

In what ways do you use Sundays to "fellowship" with others? If you don't currently do this, what could you do to help others hear God's Word or benefit from your Christian beliefs? How would doing this—sharing with others—be beneficial to your life?

_____

_____

_____

_____

_____

_____

_____

Why does God set Sunday apart? Why does He "program" what we can and cannot do on this day? Why not leave it totally up to us? Explain.

_____

_____

_____

_____

_____

_____

_____

What are some of the ways you have resisted keeping the Sabbath as Holy as God wants? After reading this chapter, what one thing would you most like to do that you're currently not doing?

_____

_____

_____

_____

_____

_____

Do you like to sing the hymns at your church? Do you belong to the church choir? Would you like to belong?

_____

_____

_____

_____

_____

_____

List your favorite Christian songs, including any Christian singer or songwriters that you most enjoy.

- _____
- _____
- _____
- _____
- _____
- _____

Is it a sin to work on Sunday? List some of the questions you'd like to have answered about this, such as:

• Is doing homework or cleaning my room considered "work"?
• Is it okay for me to work at my part-time job on Sunday—especially if it's "serving" others?
• Is it okay for a plumber or doctor to respond to an emergency call for their services?
• Is it wrong to do yard work on Sunday, since that might detract from others in the neighborhood who are resting and relaxing or spending quiet time alone or with friends?

•_____

_____

•_____

_____

•_____

_____

•_____

_____

•_____

_____

Who can you ask to help you sort through the list you just wrote down? Have you had a heart-to-heart with God about questions of this nature?

_____

_____

_____

_____

_____

_____

Do you have friends who work on Sunday? Do your parents work at their regular jobs on Sunday? If so, have you asked each one how he or she "justifies" working in the eyes of God? What about if your family really needs the extra income—would God "buy into" that reason?

_____

_____

_____

_____

_____

_____

Why does God ask that we use Sundays to come together for public worship? What is God's intent behind the law for "public" worship—why can't we just turn on the radio or television and watch a church service?

_____

_____

_____

_____

_____

_____

One purpose of God's gift of Sunday is that it be used as a time to "fellowship" with others, especially helping others learn the Word of God. In what ways can you "carry the Word" to others who cannot or do not attend church? Who in your community can benefit from your doing this?

_____

_____

_____

_____

_____

_____

In what ways does witnessing to others about your own Christian walk affect your own life? Explain.

_____

_____

_____

_____

_____

_____

In what ways do you "fellowship" on Sunday to share the word of God? If you don't do this, what could you do to help and support others in hearing God's Word or to lift their spirits?

_____

_____

_____

_____

_____

_____

"Six days shall work be done, but the Seventh day is a Sabbath of solemn rest, a holy convocation. You shall do no work on it; it is the Sabbath of the Lord in all your dwellings" (Lev. 23:3 NKJV). In this Scripture, what does "in all your dwellings" refer to?

_____

_____

_____

_____

_____

_____

"For where two or three come together in My name, there am I with them" (Matt. 18:20). What does this Scripture mean to you?

_____

_____

_____

_____

_____

_____

"Religion that God our Father accepts as pure and faultless is this: to look after orphans and widows in their distress, and to keep oneself from being polluted by the world" (James 1:27). What does this Scripture mean to you?

_____

_____

_____

_____

_____

In what ways would the world be different if everyone upheld God's fourth Commandment?

_____

_____

_____

_____

_____

_____

In what ways would the world be different if *you* upheld God's fourth Commandment?

_____

_____

_____

_____

_____

_____

How can you keep from growing complacent about upholding God's fourth Commandment?

_____

_____

_____

_____

_____

_____

The Crucifix Around My Neck

I wear a crucifix around my neck,
All day, every day, wherever I go.
No, it's not a fashion statement, not an "in thing,"
Nor is it to persuade those who say it isn't so.

I wear a crucifix around my neck,
A symbol of my faith in Christ,
Who thought of me in dying moments,
A most incredible and precious sacrifice.

I wear a crucifix around my neck,
Because he loved me from the start.
He knew my strengths, my faults, my sins,
And gave his life for me—what heart.

I wear a crucifix around my neck,
Thanking him for everything I see.
I wear it in his memory, then and now,
Because he sacrificed his life for me.

I wear a crucifix around my neck,
For his glory, I love him, I truly do.
I am not ashamed to say or show it,
In him I've found a life that's real and true.

I wear his crucifix around my neck,
It's him I choose eternally.
I am not afraid of death—nor life—because
I've secured my place in eternity.

—Laura Campanelli, 20

THE FIFTH
COMMANDMENT

*Honor your father and your mother so that you may live
long in the land the Lord your God is giving you.*

Exod. 20:12

In the previous chapter, you learned that God set Sunday apart from the other days of the week, declaring it a holy day and instructing that it be used as a day to rest, worship publicly and encourage fellowship. In this study of God's fifth Commandment, God moves on from His teaching us how to focus our love and lives around Him and begins to instruct us on how to express our love to others. As you recall from the introduction, Jesus divided his laws into two parts—love for God and love for man. The first four Commandments teach love for God, and the last six teach love for our neighbor.

The fifth Commandment has been called the "centerpiece of the Commandments" because it involves both our relationship to God and to our fellow man. Our love for others flows out of our love for God. This Commandment requests that we honor and respect our parents, as well as those in other positions of authority: "Rise in the presence of the aged, show respect for the elderly" (Lev. 19:32). As you can see by the last part of the Commandment, God shares one of the consequences for upholding His law, "so that you may live long in the land the Lord your God is giving you." Upholding the fifth Commandment shows that we revere, love and trust God, and love our "neighbors" as God loves us.

In this Commandment, the words "mother and father" are symbolic. While the phrase "mother and father" most definitely refer to your own parents, God uses these words to represent "family" in broader terms (as you'll see in the coming pages). The Commandment is broad in scope in other areas as well, demonstrating that a Christian is to think of himself or herself as a member of three families—home, state and church. God has much to say about the importance of all three.

As you already know, in each Commandment God guards something that is of the greatest importance to our welfare. Like the others, this important fifth Commandment provides direction as to what we should and should not do, this time as it relates to God's definition of "family" in the context of our responsibilities to home, state and church. It's important to have guidelines for how we are to behave anytime people come together in a group, whether at home among family members, as part of a community or when communing with our "brothers and sisters" in the world.

Is God's Fifth Commandment Still Relevant Today?

It's not a stretch to understand how this Commandment was important in days of old. In a time when people had to cope with the elements, forage for food and build their own shelter, they needed to look out for others—especially those who were dependent, such as the young, the ill and the aging. It's also understandable that when the population was expanding, specified boundaries for governing daily life—including its villages and towns—became necessary. But what about today?

How does this Commandment serve us at a time when the definition of "mother and father" has transformed as much as the family itself? Most people have been affected in some way by the chaos of separation or the heartache of divorce, causing many young people to live without a daily connection to both parents. And it is a time when abortion is frequently seen as an alternative for someone who wishes not to become a parent.

On television and in the movies, children are viewed as smaller versions of adults, and most adults are portrayed as not much more than larger versions of children. All pretty much have the same immature emotional makeup: "I want what I want, and I want it now." We live in a time in which having gray hair is more likely to be seen as "over the hill" rather than "a wise old sage." It is a time when aging seniors are more likely to live a great distance from their "upwardly mobile" children, and when seniors are likely to find themselves stashed in nursing homes with little connection to their families.

And what about family of "state"—is the fifth Commandment needed in a time when business leaders frequently sacrifice long-term goals for short-term ones? Is God satisfied with the corporate heads, state officials and elected leaders who lack the necessary integrity to lead others in "right" ways? And will God hold you and me responsible for allowing ungodly leaders to stay in their positions?

How does the fifth Commandment apply when we get an up-close and personal look at people living elsewhere, either through our own travel or via channel surfing, and fail to change the quality of their lives for the better? In what ways does this fifth Commandment lead us to address the riches and poverty that various governments induce, and the freedoms or oppressions inflicted? Can the fifth Commandment help us to sort out our world as we know it today? Does it *still* provide direction for dealing with family, church and state? Let's take a look.

Who Is "Your Father" and "Your Mother"?

Obviously, a mother and father—be they biological, adopted or surrogate parents—are "family." But this Commandment has meaning even beyond the two, three or four adults we call "Mom" and "Dad." Consider how Jesus referred to the wider sense of family. When Jesus was speaking to the multitudes someone said to him, "Your mother and brothers are standing outside, wanting to speak to you." Jesus replied, "Who is my mother, and who are my brothers?" Pointing to his disciples, he said, "Here are my mother and my brothers. For whoever does the will of my Father in heaven is my brother and sister and mother" (Matt. 12:47–50).

In 1 Timothy 5:1–3, we learn that "family" has an even larger membership: "Do not rebuke an older man harshly, but exhort him as if he were your father. Treat younger men as brothers, older women as mothers, and younger women as sisters, with absolute purity. Give proper recognition to those widows who are really in need." Scripture even explains a bit of our responsibility to "family" by saying, "But if a widow has children or grandchildren, these should learn first of all to put their religion into practice by caring for their own family and so repaying their parents and grandparents, for this is pleasing to God. . . . If any woman who is a believer has widows in her family, she should help them and not let the church be burdened with them, so that the church can help those widows who are really in need" (1 Tim. 5:4, 16).

Regardless of their origin, parents are incredibly important to God—and He expects us to hold them in the highest regard. But He also asks a great deal of them, as well. For starters, God expects parents to be leaders in their homes. Let's see what this means.

Family Leadership: Who "Runs the Show" at Your House?

The fifth Commandment is not only for our own good, but for the sake of those with whom we share our lives. Imagine if there were no leadership in your home, or if everyone did his or her own thing regardless of how that affected the other members. Certainly this can result in divorce when one or both parents place their own desires above the needs and well-being of all family members. Even children can bring dissension in the family. Perhaps you've seen the effects yourself when one member of the family starts looking out only for his or her own well-being or special interests. This happened to sixteen-year-old Dana Hartford, who tells of her ordeal: "When my older sister was seventeen, she decided no one should tell her what to do. To make her point, she was belligerent and uncooperative, not only to our parents but to me as well. She only wanted what she wanted, and she didn't care how it affected anyone else in the family. Our home was turned into a battlefield. We could no longer act like a family or plan things because we couldn't count on her. It was like my sister was running the whole show. Everyone in the whole family was miserable because of her."

As Dana learned, in order to create family harmony, each family member has responsibilities and common courtesies that must be followed so that there is order in the household.

While the fifth Commandment assigns the leadership of children to the adults, it then gives children instructions on honoring and praying for their parents. All of this has bearing on the happiness of the "institution" of family.

The fifth Commandment's instructions for parents are to pray for their children; house, feed and clothe them; protect them from harm and danger; comfort them in sorrow; and watch over them in sickness. Their duties include nurturing their children, as well as guiding and instructing them in the Word of God. Such is the charge that God gives parents. So what if parents do not do these things—are children given license to be angry with and disobey their parents? Not according to God, who says, "Cursed is the man who dishonors his father or his mother" (Deut. 27:16).

What Does God Expect of You— Your Parents' Children?

God provides direction to you, the children, as well, regardless of how young or old you are. God asks that children honor, serve, obey, love and esteem their parents. In fact, children are even charged with protecting the "good name" of their parents. Regardless of what you personally think of your parents— whether you think they are "good" parents or not—God asks that children pray for their parents and for themselves. God calls for obedience when you feel your parents are wrong; God calls for respect even if you feel your parents do not deserve it; and God calls for loyalty even when your parents seem to be unreasonable. Does this mean that parents are always right or always do what is best? No. But God doesn't instruct us to obey only when we think they're right! He doesn't leave this judgment up to the kids—regardless of how old and wise we are! We are to honor, respect and obey our parents—and we are to do this because God says so. Maybe this is why God asks kids—young and old alike—to bring their concerns about their parents to Him. After all, God is our Father, too—our Heavenly Father.

Why Life in the Family IS the "Real World"

God knows that what we learn by being a member of a family is vital to living among others in the "real world." Maybe that's why we humans have within our nature a desire to be with others. How many of your friends would rather stay alone in their rooms as opposed to being invited by others to spend time and fellowship with them? Every now and then, we get a little tired of always being around others—but not too often. Mostly we prefer the company of others.

The more time we spend with others, the better we understand the rules for getting along. This is a good thing. No one likes to be with selfish, self-centered, arrogant, "it's-all-about-me" kind of people. This is another reason why learning to be a "member" of your family at home is a good thing. For example, in addition to learning how to share and look out for the comfort and well-being of others, one of the values your parents are trying to instill is to have a healthy respect for authority. Authority teaches self-control, patience and tolerance, among other things—all essential qualities to living life on your own and being with others. Having a mind-set for looking out for others and a heart generous enough to care about the comfort of others are the hallmarks of understanding that you're sharing your time here on Earth with others, and for a reason.

Being a member of a family teaches you all these things and more. This is why being a member of a family IS the real world. What you learn there is what you will carry into the world each day—starting with today. So take a good look at your family and see their well-being as important as your own. Learning how to share and be responsible in pulling your weight helps cure the syndrome: "I am the important person on Earth. The universe—especially this family—centers around ME." Fifteen-year-old Michelle McCabe saw this same attitude in her friend, Raynelle.

> It seems to me that my friend, Raynelle, runs her family. She always seems to get her way, no matter what. And it's not like she's grateful for it; she's always ragging on her parents, always complaining. She's always wanting something, and it's not like her family can afford everything her little heart desires. I've been to her house, and I know that her family lives modestly. Still, Raynelle dresses in the latest fashions, always has a few dollars in her purse and doesn't think twice about buying new CDs or makeup or whatever. She's a bit snobbish, really, and acts entitled, like she deserves anything she wants. Raynelle is in four of my classes—which is one of the reasons we hang out a little, but of all my friends, she is the most overbearing, the most difficult one to consider as a "good friend." It's tiring to be around her for very long—and it's because she thinks of herself before anyone else. If it weren't that she was a good student and because we sometimes study together, I wouldn't stay friends with her.
>
> **—Michelle McCabe, 15**

Do you have friends who, like Raynelle, suffer from an "attitude disorder"? If so, you'll note that this attitude usually is accompanied by arrogance and detesting one's parents. It's pretty easy to tell who among your friends feels this way about their homes and family members: Young people who do not respect their parents also show little to no respect for teachers, coaches, pastors or others in authority positions. They have placed themselves and their desires above all else, and they care about little else other than themselves.

Being a member of a family is in the best interest of everyone. And so God guards it with what my daughter Jennifer calls "the nesting Commandment." By honoring their parents, children show that they love God and become a blessing to their parents.

What Does God Say About the Responsibility of Your Parents?

As you've figured out by now, God's laws are so perfectly thought out that they benefit everybody—which is why this Commandment is not a one-way street. Parents have obligations, too—in fact, far more than their children do! Besides caring for their children's physical needs, parents are expected to live a life characterized by integrity, honesty, responsibility and faith in God. They are instructed to earn and be worthy of their children's love and obedience. Prayer and family devotions are a part of their responsibility. And they are to teach their children self-control. God goes so far as to ask parents to correct children when they are not being obedient, saying, "Do not withhold discipline from a child" (Prov. 23:13). This does not give parents a license for dominance, being unfair or cruel. To parents, God lectures, "Fathers, do not exasperate your children; instead, bring them up in the training and instruction of the Lord" (Eph. 6:4). Most of all, God expects parents to teach their children about God and to demonstrate—through their own behavior—God's love, as we learn in Proverbs 22:6: "Train a child in the way he should go, and when he is old, he will not turn from it."

Five Ways to Honor Your Parents and God

1. *Love your parents.* The older you get, the more you want to take control of your life. That is as it should be. Still, listen to what your parents have to say. Allow them to shape your character—to help you always to see life from the eyes of your heart, and to learn about God's love so that you will want to be a person who walks with God. Maybe your parents do that already. Maybe they don't know how to do that; maybe they're still trying to come to terms with their own hurts and wounds from the past. Maybe their own lives are filled with chaos, and it spills over into your own, making for a difficult relationship between the two of you. If this is the case, ask for God's guidance in loving and honoring your parents. Have you ever asked God to lead you into a better relationship with your parents? God wants you to, and it's sure to give you insight on how to make your family life better.

 Do all you can to love your parents. Do all you can to create a happy home for all the members of your family. Don't expect your parents to be perfect just because they're older. Each day you get out of bed is the first day they've had the opportunity to be your parents on that day. It may be difficult to believe, but parents are learning as they go, too. Does this absolve them of the responsibility to be effective parents? No, but it can help you see them as being mere humans. Do all you can to create a relationship "for the long haul." Hopefully, you and your parents will have a long life upon the Earth and many years to keep working at perfecting the love between you. As a child, I was certain that God had made a mistake by dropping me off at the doorstep of my family. As a teen, I remember looking over my family and saying to God, "How did I get stuck with these people?" Like many young people, I coped and then planned my "escape"—which, for me, was to go off to college just as soon as I could.

Like others my age, I felt my parents were too strict, but it wasn't long after I left home that I could see the benefits of all I had learned from them. It didn't take too many days until I felt the pangs of missing them, and I realized just how fully I loved them. I believe it was right around age twenty that I began to understand how incredibly lucky I was to have been "dropped off" in my family, knowing God had known best after all. Luckily, with this early realization, my parents and I shared nearly four decades of mutual love and admiration. I lost my mother two years ago. Several months ago, at the age of eighty-two, my daddy died. I can tell you firsthand that I never have and never will again experience the magnitude of love and acceptance that I received from my parents. It was, and remains—with the exception of my relationship with God—the most complete and loving relationship of any I've ever known. In all of my adult years, talking and being with either my mother or father made all else in life unimportant. To be one of their children was the greatest gift I've ever been given. To be without them now is the greatest loss I've yet to experience. Such is the power of the bond we can form with our parents. I wish it for you, and I hope you will work to make it so.

You are young and it can seem like parents are "behind the times," too strict or not "hip" enough. Even so, go for the relationship. Next to asking God to walk with you in life, it will be the biggest "learning lesson" you ever will have. It can also be the most satisfying and the most soothing to your heart. And know that your own future children will feel just as you do sometimes—that "the parents" are "behind the times," too strict or not "hip" enough! That's just the way it works! Trust me, God has thought all this through. He's got a plan—and you're in the thick of it!

Someone once said, "Our lives are shaped by those who love us and those who refuse to love us." How very true. Regardless of the way you see some of your friends treat their parents, vow to love and honor your own. Ask God to grant you the peaceful and loving heart that makes you a joy and blessing to your parents.

2. *Obey the house rules—and look for the love behind them.* It's always difficult to color within the lines, but sometimes it's the only way to get a picture to turn out the way it's supposed to be! Likewise, when you follow the rules your parents have set, you are more likely to be safe and to feel like you are loved. You will see your own (good) character emerge.

What if you feel the rules are too strict or out of line? Then try this: Think about each rule, and then write each one down. Next, write out what you feel is the reason for each of the rules. Then, draw a line, making two columns. In one column, list all the possible benefits for following the rules, and in the next column, list all the ways the rule protects you or serves you. Now study it. Do you still wish for some change? If so, have a talk with your parents and see if they are willing to give you a little more "rope"—such as a longer curfew, more time with friends, and so on.

The bottom line is that parents enjoy it when their children learn and grow and change. Most all parents look forward to their children learning to "stand on their own two feet." Being able to make wise choices helps your parents see that you are not only growing up, but growing wise. Often the trick to peaceful coexistence is talking things out, as seventeen-year-old Shannon Boston learned.

Beginning in junior high, the older I got, the dumber my parents got. While they had once been the most wonderful parents, now suddenly they were oppressive, overbearing, ridiculous and overprotective. We fought constantly over things like how I dressed, how I wore my hair, my grades, my friends. Then I got caught with alcohol in my locker at school. Although my parents were alarmed as well as disappointed in me, they were also fair in the consequences they levied for my actions. They didn't treat me like I was a really terrible person who needed to be punished; they focused their concern on my knowing the dangers of drinking, and the fine line between using and becoming chemically dependent. So now I see my parents' strictness as their sincere caring about me. I thought I knew so much; now I see how much I needed—and still need—their guidance.

—Shannon Boston, 17

3. *Learn to be a good communicator—and ask God to sit in on family discussions.* Because you are getting old enough to make decisions of your own, you may very well need to talk with your parents about what the rules are and how to cocreate new ones. If you still need to work on discussion and negotiation skills, don't wait for your parents to learn and apply them. Get busy and do this for yourself. Start by being a good listener. Learn how to express yourself in ways that assure you will be listened to and taken seriously. Ask God to sit in on things. Learn to say, "Let's pray about this, and talk again"—which is exactly what Greg Williams, fifteen, learned made all the difference in his relationship with his parents.

I used to get really frustrated with my parents because they put a limit on the time I could spend on the phone, and they were constantly checking to see what I'd been looking at on the Internet. I wanted to be trusted—because I am trustworthy. It wasn't until I asked God to help my parents trust me at face value that they did. But it has made all the difference. I would say to anyone, why think you can do it alone? I mean, there's a reason behind everything. Use every discussion as a way to learn about God's intention for your life. Don't leave Him out of the picture. Doing that is just plain dumb.

—Greg Williams, 15

4. *Be appreciative and practice saying "thank you."* Think about the times when someone appreciated sincerely something you've done and told you so. Didn't that make you feel good about yourself? Didn't the fact that you'd been praised bond you to the person who expressed satisfaction? Quite often, parents don't get the praise and thanksgiving they deserve. Just because parents are "supposed" to care for you, don't neglect to show your gratitude. Make it your honor—as much as it is your obligation to God—to show gratitude for all your parents do for you. This can be simple, such as, "Dad/Mom, thank you for taking me to school this morning." Or "Thank you for being my dad (or mom)." Or "Thank you for cheering me on at my game yesterday. It helped me to feel more confident." An attitude of gratitude is pleasing to your parents. Moreover, it is pleasing to God.

5. *Look out for your siblings.* On my parents' fiftieth wedding anniversary, they gathered us kids together for a dinner. Immediately following the meal, they handed each of us a half sheet of paper upon which they had typed a "message" for us to always keep—words they wanted us to take to heart. It said, "Please always love each other. Take care and look after each other. Raise God-loving children. If you do this, we will feel that we have been, in some way, good parents." This was followed by the following Scripture: "If your brother sins against you, go and show him his fault, just between the two of you. If

he listens to you, you have won your brother over. If he will not listen, take one or two others along so that 'every matter may be established by the testimony of two or three witnesses.' . . . I tell you, that if two of you on Earth agree about anything you ask for, it will be done for you by My Father in heaven. . . . Then Peter came to Jesus and asked, 'Lord, how many times shall I forgive my brother when he sins against me? Up to seven times?' Jesus answered, 'I tell you, not seven times, but seventy-seven times'" (Matt. 18:15–16, 19, 21–22).

What we children learned was that of all the things our parents had done in their roles as parents, they considered that our loving each other, and caring for each other the way God intended, was the mark of their having succeeded as parents. If one of us were to step out of line, we were to go and convince that person to come back to the fold. "A healthy family always claims each other," they told us. "No matter what, and under all conditions, whether it be in times of celebration or chaos, love each other and take care of each other." That little slip of paper has remained so important to each of us children that we each still have it—for some of us, framed and on a wall. Amazing what God-guided love can do!

Most parents want their children to love, look after and always "be right" with their siblings. Do this because you love your parents. Do this because you want to grow in love for your brothers and sisters. Do this because you love God. It is because of His love that you are learning, day by day, the importance of loving all His children, everywhere.

The "Family" of Government: What Does God Say Is Its Duty to Its People?

Did you think that the government was thought up by us earthlings? Not so. Scripture is filled with God's mandates for how the "state" must be organized and how it is to conduct itself in the "fair dealings" (treatment) of His people. God does not want us to look at government as being an impersonal entity. God wants us to see the government as an extension of our willingness to care about and for each other—to look after His children's well-being.

Who is the "state"? The state is the "larger family"—meaning all those who "live in the land." This may be a city, a town or the geographic boundaries of a state. According to God, the duty of a government is to govern in accordance with the laws of the land. It's easy to see that, without this, there would be neither law nor order. So God directs that government is to work for the people. Does God have something to say to our litigious society? You bet: "Settle matters quickly with your adversary who is taking you to court. Do it while you are still with him on the way, or he may hand you over to the judge, and the judge may hand you over to the officer, and you may be thrown into prison" (Matt. 5:25).

Ideally, it's up to the people to decide what form of government they wish to be under. And so the responsibility of the government should be that it faithfully work for the welfare of the people according to the laws it has set forth. It is the duty of this government to be honest and just, and to protect those who follow its laws, as well as to punish those who do not. Does God demand that the rulers be just, impartial and trustworthy? You bet. He demands it: "He does not bear the sword for nothing. He is God's servant" (Rom. 13:4). If you're thinking that God expects us to pray for our leaders and for our government, you would be correct.

To the citizen God says, "Everyone must submit himself to the governing authorities" (Rom. 13:1). So what if the leader (hence the government) is corrupt? Are you willing to pray for leaders such as Saddam Hussein? And what if the government asks us to do that which the Word of God forbids? Above all, God expects us to obey Him over all others, saying, "Give to Caesar what is Caesar's, and to God what is God's" (Matt. 22:21). If you take this one step further, you will see that incorporated into this Commandment is a promise to nations, as well. While the promise in this Commandment was especially given to Israel, it is also a promise to all nations who uphold its meaning. A nation that honors fathers and mothers because it fears and loves God—because it "walks righteously"—will be strong morally and physically. The individual shares in the safety and blessings that doing so brings.

What Does the Fifth Commandment Say About Your Obligation to the Government?

What does it mean to honor the state, and in what ways can you personally do your part? List all the ways you can think of that show you do all you can to see that the "state" is as good as it can be. Go ahead and do this now on page 152.

Did you create a long list, or did you only list a few? As a young adult, there are many ways you can make a difference in honoring the "state." Practically speaking, honoring the state means the obvious, like not breaking the laws against shoplifting, stealing and killing. But it also means to obey the laws of the land, such as no speeding or running stop signs. It means paying taxes that we owe and not cheating. It means not throwing trash out the windows of your car, thereby marring the countryside. It means serving in the military if the draft ever should be reinstated. It means praying for our leaders that they would have "the mind of Christ" as they make decisions in governing our country. It means doing your part to support the country so that we can function harmoniously as a "family." And more.

The following young people say these are some of the ways they uphold the "family" of government.

Four Ways You Can Honor the "Family" of Government—A Word from Your Peers

1. Value freedom, and don't take it for granted.

Since September 11, I'm far more aware of how lucky I am to live in a country that values freedom. I feel so blessed and thank God every day for the freedoms I enjoy. Now when I sing the National Anthem, I think about how God has blessed our country, and pledging allegiance is more of a prayer. Since my awareness has been heightened, I'm a better citizen. I'm more courteous to others, I'm more polite, and I speak up about the importance of freedom and everything related to it. I pray with all my heart for our soldiers who are risking their God-given lives so that we can maintain the freedoms we enjoy. And I have much to say about governments who do not create freedoms for their people. I have become, I've discovered, an activist.

—Jonathan Bridges, 14

2. Obey the laws.

I just got my driver's license so now I'm aware of more things about driving. One of the surprises has been how concerned I've become about how my actions affect others. For example, last week I changed lanes without checking my blind spot and nearly ran a driver off the road. Speed limits, traffic lights and stop signs are put there for our safety, and when I disregard them, I put others in danger. That's not what I want to do. Therefore, I count obeying the traffic laws as part of what I can do to keep our communities safe, which is one way to uphold God's fifth Commandment.

—Bethany Oglethorpe, 16

3. Vote for those who stand for the values of justice, fairness and honesty.

> *When I look at the leaders of the world, I know their desire to lead others didn't just hatch overnight. Probably it started when they were in their early or midteens. I know several of the kids at school who are always running for class president, student body president or some other position where they can lead. I think these are the very people who, in later years, will run for city government or state government or be an elected official somewhere. So I take their "platforms" seriously. If someone says he or she is going to work to make something happen, I hold that person's "feet to the fire," so to speak—I let the person know that I voted for him or her based on that promise, and that I expect the person to follow through. I no longer vote for someone simply because that person is my friend or more popular than someone else who may be running for office. I take my voting power seriously. I think it's exactly what this mandate from God is about—and it's one of our obligations to the family of state.*

> **—Jennifer Hanson, 17**

4. Pray for the leaders of your country.

> *My favorite book is* Lord of the Flies. *A group of little boys survive a plane crash and are marooned on an island. Without realizing what they are doing, the first thing they do is to set up their own government with rules and responsibilities for everybody. But because there is no one to enforce adherence, the government begins to break down and chaos breaks loose— at its worst, they begin killing each other. Those little boys represent who we are without God, and the anarchy shows what we'd be like without government. God in His love and wisdom gave us government.*

> **—Dan Deerborne, 20**

What Does God Say About the Obligation of the Church to You—and You to the Church?

Because we recognize God as the source and center of life, we gather in His name. There are some who believe they needn't go to church, a temple or holy place to pay tribute to God. Some people believe God hears them no matter where they are, and so that is good enough—wherever they are, they are already with God. This is not God's interpretation. As you recall from the previous chapter, in His fourth Commandment, God asks that we use Sundays specifically to come together for public worship. This can encourage and support others in their Christian walk. When we lift our voices in praise to Him, side by side with others, we encourage others to know God more fully. This is the power of belonging to a church—and how doing so serves your Christian walk. You must give back.

The church is a spiritual family. As a "church" family, we look out for the spiritual "health" of each other. It is the duty of a Christian to pray for the church, along with its pastors, teachers and other workers. We are charged with knowing the functions of our church, and, moreover, we are expected to support the church and its goals—such as providing Sunday school and bringing the Word of God to those who cannot attend, but would like to—such as the ill. We are each to do this to the best of our ability, and in accordance to the gifts and talents God has individually bestowed.

The following young adults suggest some ways we can honor the family of the church.

Four Ways You Can Honor the "Family" of Church—A Word from Your Peers

1. Go to church.

> *My parents have always taken me to church; I've never had a choice about going, and I think that's good. Because I've been*

going forever, it feels as natural as going to school. I've grown up knowing God, but each Sunday I learn something new. Some kids want to quit going when they get to be teenagers, but that's not good because that's when life starts to get complicated. I know there are lots of handy excuses if you want to justify not going to services: "Some people there are hypocrites; they only go to see their friends." "They always ask for money." "I don't like the music." "The lady behind me sang too loudly." What if you used the same excuses about the school football game? "They wouldn't let me in for free; they insisted that I buy a ticket." "I saw some people there who don't even like football; they just went to be with their friends." "I don't like the school's fight song." "The guy behind me yelled too loudly." Would these reasons keep you away from the game? Probably not! So why would you let them keep you out of church? If I stopped feeding my cat, she would die. And if I stopped going to church, I would die spiritually. I need spiritual food as well as what's in the refrigerator at home.

—Gretchen Ashmore, 13

2. Tithe.

I tithe not only because God expects me to, but because our sharing what we have with others is a part of God's plan to continue spreading the Word of God. I have some friends who say that getting a prescription from the pharmacy for an elderly person is doing God's work. While that's true, God expects us to give money directly to the church so that it can fulfill its goals and obligations to any outreach ministries it has. So I'm faithful in giving my share. I consider it an obligation to God, one that I'm okay fulfilling.

—Christina Salazar, 16

3. Accept Jesus as Lord and Savior of your life.

Last year was the first time I ever went to church. A friend invited me to go with him, and several weeks later, I accepted Christ into my life. To say I've never been the same would be an understatement to say the least! My life was boring, and, I'd have to say, kind of meaningless. But now, I'm on fire! I have purpose. I have direction. I have energy. I love life. Now my church is like family to me. I go now because it is the "juice" I need to keep me going. To keep me healthy. To keep me mentally and morally strong. Thank you, God, for that.

—**Dwayne Carter, 17**

4. Hang out with other Christians.

My church youth group is the center of my social life. I've found all my best friends there because we share the same values and goals—our faith in Jesus Christ. We study, learn and pray together, but we also play together; some of my best memories have been going to camps, amusement parks and skiing with my youth group. Because we all share the same faith, I don't have to worry about being pressured to do wrong things, and I can count on my friends to make sure that I don't get off track either. I can't imagine life without my Christian friends.

—**Doug Donovan, 15**

Family: A Brand of Love Unparalleled to Any Other

As you've learned in this chapter, God takes great care to let us know the importance of journeying with others, and so He sets out a Commandment to govern our actions with one another, beginning with family. My mother used to say, "Oh, family! So good to see them come; so good to see them go!" She was talking, of course, about the fact that being with our family members is always loving, but always taxing, as well. God knew we'd be having these feelings, of course, which is why He took such care when crafting this incredibly important Commandment.

It is within our families that all of real life is played out. With them we let our hair down, relax and feel free to express our deepest needs, greatest fears and infinite hopes. It is with them that we feel able to discuss our hurts, pains and wounds. It is with them that we express feelings of love. After all, these are the people with whom we have laughed and cried, cooked and shared meals, and played and fought on a daily basis over many years. It is with these people that we can be ourselves. They've seen us at our arrogant best and, most assuredly, at our worst and lowest moments. And still, they love us. Home is where we turn to when we need to fill up our tanks with the brand of love that family reserve only for each other. It is a love unparalleled to any other.

Yes, the bonds of family are important to our lives. The strength of character we gain there will be our passport to living successfully in the world. Asking God to walk with us and guide us as we learn to love and appreciate each person in our families will be the mortar for the rooms we build within our hearts so that we have space to love others. How are you doing learning these things? Have you learned the importance of family—or are you still acting like it's "them against me"? Have you come to the conclusion that you're old enough and wise enough now to share love with your family in ways that help them heal wounds of their own, and that create happiness that they can never get from any source other than you? Take to heart the advice in Philippians 2:4, "Each of you should look not only to your own interests, but also to the interests of others."

Ask God to help you create this within the context of your family.

YOUR PERSONAL JOURNAL

In what ways does God's fifth Commandment apply to your life today? In what ways is it still relevant?

_____

_____

_____

_____

_____

_____

Think about your lifestyle. In what ways do you break the fifth Commandment?

_____

_____

_____

_____

_____

_____

In what ways do you uphold God's fifth Commandment?

_____

_____

_____

_____

_____

_____

Why is the fifth Commandment called the centerpiece of the Commandments?

_____

_____

_____

_____

_____

_____

The fifth Commandment requests that we honor and respect our parents and not provoke them to anger. What do you think is meant by "do not provoke them to anger"? Give an example of a time you did this. Why did you provoke them? Did you know at the time this is what you were doing? Did you provoke them intentionally? How did you feel about the way things turned out?

_____

_____

_____

_____

_____

_____

Having read this chapter, if you were having a heart-to-heart with your family, what is the one thing you would like to tell them about the importance of family relationships? Why would this be important to you?

_____

_____

_____

_____

_____

_____

According to God's fifth law, children are not given much license to be angry with their parents. "Cursed is the man who dishonors his father or his mother" (Deut. 27:16). What is God's reasoning for making this demand?

_____

_____

_____

_____

_____

_____

_____

Do you follow the rules your parents have set? Do you feel they are too strict? As you did earlier in this chapter, write out each rule, and then next to it, write down the reason for the rule. Then list all the possible benefits for following the rules, followed by the ways the rules protect you.

• Rule: _____

Benefit of rule to me: _____

_____

Benefit of rule to the family: _____

_____

• Rule: _____
Benefit of rule to me: _____

_____

Benefit of rule to the family: _____

_____

• Rule: _____
Benefit of rule to me: _____

_____

Benefit of rule to the family: _____

_____

• Rule: _____
Benefit of rule to me: _____

_____

Benefit of rule to the family: _____

_____

God considers "the state" as a part of the "larger family." In what ways do you think of the state as an extension of family?

_____

_____

_____

_____

_____

The duty of a government is to govern in accordance with the "laws of the land," but it is up to the people to decide what form of government they wish to be under. Do you think we have an obligation to each other to vote? Do you think we have an obligation to be conscious about our vote—to see that those voted into office are capable of being in their position? Explain your reasoning.

_____

_____

_____

_____

_____

_____

God says that it is the *duty* of the government to be honest and just, and to protect those who follow its laws—as well as to punish those who do not. What do you think this means in terms of a government starting a war or punishing those who break the "laws of the land"?

_____

_____

_____

_____

_____

God demands that all rulers be just, impartial and trustworthy. What does He have to say about those who do not rule in accordance with these mandates?

_____

_____

_____

_____

_____

What can you, a young adult, do if a school or community leader is corrupt? Have you been involved with the government at your school? Why or why not? Do you consider it an aspect of your personality or a responsibility to God to be involved in the way your school and community is run?

_____

_____

_____

_____

_____

_____

What would God say to you or anyone who said something to the effect: "I don't like the rules for our student center, but I'm too shy to change them"?

_____

_____

_____

_____

_____

_____

"Settle matters quickly with your adversary who is taking you to court. Do it while you are still with him on the way, or he may hand you over to the judge, and the judge may hand you over to the officer, and you may be thrown into prison" (Matt. 5:25).

What does this mean to you? Do you think it happens frequently? Ask some attorneys you know (or can speak with) about how often they see this happening. Also ask each attorney if he or she were aware that doing this is a mandate from God.

_____

_____

_____

_____

_____

God says we are to pray for our leaders and our government. Do you do this? Do you consider it important to pray for leaders around the world? Do you think prayer could help us improve the conditions of the world?

_____

_____

_____

_____

_____

_____

What does it mean to honor the state? List all the ways you can think of, such as obeying the speed limit.

_____

_____

_____

_____

_____

_____

If you were an elected president of the United States, what stance would you take with leaders such as Saddam Hussein? Would you pray for guidance in making your decision? Explain.

_____

_____

_____

_____

_____

_____

God sees the church as our spiritual family. Do you see your church through God's eyes? Explain.

_____

_____

_____

_____

_____

God says that it is the duty of a Christian to pray for the church, along with its pastors, teachers and other workers. Do you pray for your church in this way?

_____

_____

_____

_____

_____

_____

God says it is the duty of a Christian to support the church in its goals to provide Sunday school to the young and bring the Word of God to those who cannot be in attendance. In what ways do you support the goals and obligations of the church?

_____

_____

_____

_____

_____

_____

God tells us public worship is important because it enables us to encourage and support each other in learning God's Word. Besides your own congregation, in what ways do you worship "publicly"?

_____

_____

_____

_____

_____

Do you think it is our obligation to support and assist each other in all the ways we can? Explain.

_____

_____

_____

_____

_____

Are you happy with your family life? Is God happy with the ways you contribute to your family? Explain.

_____

_____

_____

_____

_____

_____

What two things do you do that show God you are helping your family to be loving and happy?

_____

_____

_____

_____

_____

_____

What does "to serve and obey your parents" mean to you? In what ways do you see yourself doing this?

_____

_____

_____

_____

_____

_____

Have you ever provoked anyone in an authority role—be it your parents, a teacher, coach, police officer or someone else?

Why did this happen? How did things turn out? What did you learn?

_____

_____

_____

_____

_____

In what ways would the world be different if everyone upheld God's fifth Commandment?

_____

_____

_____

_____

_____

In what ways would the world be different if *you* upheld God's fifth Commandment?

_____

_____

_____

_____

_____

How can you keep from growing complacent about upholding God's fifth Commandment?

_____

_____

_____

THE SIXTH
COMMANDMENT

You shall not murder.

Exod. 20:13

I n the previous chapter, you learned that God instructed us to honor our fathers and mothers—so our days are "long in the land." The sixth Commandment is about living long, as well, but this time as it relates to the preservation of life. Because human life has eternal value to God, He created a law to protect human life against willful destruction.

This "value-of-life" Commandment has implications beyond taking the life of another. Certainly we're NOT to take the life of a fellow human being, but the Commandment protects beyond the number of days in which we're given to breathe. This sixth Commandment also declares that we are to care about others— and to the degree that we do them no bodily harm, nor cause them any suffering. We are told to help and befriend each other in every need. "Greater love has no one than this, that he lay down his life for his friends" (John 15:13).

Not only does God call for the protection of human life in His sixth law, but we are informed of the consequences if we disobey: "Whoever sheds the blood of man, by man shall his blood be shed. For in the image of God has God made man" (Gen. 9:6). Out of reverence, love and trust for God, and because we love others as God loves us, we abide by His Commandment.

Is God's Sixth Commandment Still Relevant Today?

As with all the Commandments, God guards something that is of great importance to our well-being. It is not too difficult to understand that God is looking out for our interests when He commands that someone not murder us. God also tells us we're to not cause each other suffering—be it physical pain or emotional duress. Considering some of the brutality that existed in days of yore—from the very real possibility of being thrown into a gladiator's den where being a meal for lions was a real probability, to the fate (as was true for Jesus) of being nailed to a cross with a wreath of thorns thrust onto your head—it's understandable how the sixth Commandment was direly needed in such merciless times.

But what about in modern civilization? How does this law speak to us today, an era in which some countries openly wage war against each other, and "ethnic cleansing" is known to occur? How does this ancient Commandment apply to terrorism, such as the brutal attack of September 11, in which its perpetrators justified the lives of those murdered as a jihad, or holy war? And what about hate crimes—certainly many of our streets are not safe from gang wars and shoot-outs.

How shall we apply the Commandment to crimes against race, creed, color and sexual differences, or as the multitude of school shootings suggest, against those who inflict pain or death upon others because they feel different, excluded or suffer from feelings of alienation? How does the Commandment sort out or justify the destruction of life, be it on death row, through suicide or an abortion? Does it offer any guidelines to keep drunk drivers off the road and drug dealers off the streets? Does the Commandment speak to the school bully tormenting the timid? Let's take a look.

The Love Behind the Law: To God, Each Human Life Has Eternal Value

The love behind God's sixth law is this: *To God, all human life is sacred; each soul has eternal value.*

God's reasoning is straightforward. We each are God's creation: "So God created man in his own image, in the image of God

He created him; male and female He created them" (Gen. 1:27). Rightly so, God declares that each and every one of us belong to Him. A crime against another person's life is a crime against God. That alone should make us stop and think about inflicting death or emotional duress upon another. Consider what is at stake for God: When God looks upon His children, He sees the eternal possibilities. When you look at a good friend, perhaps your first "take" is "good friend; happy person; smart; makes me laugh; we like to spend time together," or something to that effect. While we see attributes or qualities (good or bad), God sees a soul when he gazes upon His children. *In each of us, God sees the untold possibility for each of our lives to be with Him throughout time and eternity.*

Under God, each of us shares the same birthright: We all have the opportunity for companionship with God. By living according to the Commandments set forth for our welfare, we each have a right to understand and take the walk that leads to being reunited with God. God wants each of His children to know eternal life.

God is serious about each life; no one must destroy or harm in any way that which is His. Should we fear for ourselves if we transgress against God? Scripture provides ample evidence: "This day I call heaven and Earth as witnesses against you that I have set before you life and death, blessings and curses. Now choose life, so that you and your children may live and that you may love the Lord your God, listen to His voice, and hold fast to Him. For the Lord is your life and he will give you many years in the land he swore to give to your fathers, Abraham, Isaac and Jacob" (Deut. 30:19–20). Likewise, he is serious about banishing anyone who would take the life of one of His children: "For the morning is the same to them as the shadow of death. . . . Their portion should be cursed in the Earth. . . . The worm should feed sweetly on him; he should be remembered no more, and wickedness should be broken like a tree" (Job 24:17–20 NKJV).

Like God, we, too, are to value life as sacred, knowing that each life begins as a gift from Him. Therefore, we have an obligation to God to care for His children, so they may come to know God and also share in the birthright of life everlasting.

Does God Make a Distinction Between *Murder* and *Killing*?

Notice that the Commandment is more accurately translated as *"You shall not murder"* rather than *"You shall not kill."* If God had said the latter, then his explicit instructions to the Israelites as to how they were to annihilate the pagan tribes who were occupying the Promised Land would have been completely contradictory to his own instructions. What does this mean for us, living in a time in which our world is uncertain and volatile? Again, Scripture provides insight: ". . . a time for war and a time for peace" (Eccles. 3:8), and ". . . a time to kill and a time to heal" (Eccles. 3:3). And so we can conclude that, under certain circumstances, killing within the context of war does not violate the sixth Commandment. Rather, soldiers protect the freedom and safety of the citizens of a country and of the generations who will follow behind. Justified war, then, falls under the category of self-defense and is justified under God's laws. But this does not mean we are to regard war as something to be taken lightly: "Wisdom is better than weapons of war" (Eccles. 9:18), and "Make plans by seeking advice; if you wage war, obtain guidance" (Prov. 20:18).

Who, then, is a murderer? Is it only the person who kills intentionally, as in shooting someone to death? Or is it also applied to that person who, while driving recklessly or under the influence of drugs or alcohol, causes an accident in which someone loses his or her life? What if life is lost through assisted suicide or abortion? These are serious and troubling questions for

mankind. Certainly, they are exactly the kinds of "moral" judg-
ments that are worth your debate among family and friends and
within your youth group.

God's Word: A Moral Compass for Evaluating Moral Judgments

Luckily, we have God's Word to provide us with a moral compass for evaluating ways in which we inflict hurt, punish or take
the life of another. What we learn is that God doesn't easily
excuse us or let us off the hook. "If you suffer, it should not be as
a murderer or thief or any other kind of criminal, or even as a
meddler" (1 Pet. 4:15). God even has words for those of us whose
"evildoings" remain locked in our heads. Says God, he who is
angry with his brother also is guilty of murder. "You have heard
that it was said to the people long ago, 'Do not murder, and anyone who murders will be subject to judgment.' But I tell you that
anyone who is angry with his brother will be subject to judgment'" (Matt. 5:21–22). In the sight of God, hatred is the root of
murder. It may never make us criminals, but it makes us sin
against God.

God wants us to "clean house" on all thinking that is "hateful." God wants us to know that even neglecting to help others
who need our support is, in fact, a selfish cruelty—and a sin
against His Commandment. As future leaders of the world, you
might even speculate as to the broader application of "murder."
What might it mean for those who produce, sell and/or adver-
tise cigarettes, liquor or other harmful substances? What about
those who promote things, such as pornography, that destroy a
person's spirit or desire to serve God? Isn't this, too, a sin against
this Commandment? God goes so far as to say that even the
motives for doing evil fall under the umbrella of murder:
"Anyone who hates his brother is a murderer" (1 John 3:15). The

consequences are dire: "You know that no murderer has eternal life in him" (1 John 3:15).

Suicide: Is It a Sin?

Again, to God our lives are precious: They are holy, sacred, blessed and consecrated. "God's temple is sacred, and you are that temple" (1 Cor. 3:17). But what if a person has an incurable disease or a terminal illness, making life seem unbearable? Might that be grounds for ending one's own suffering? God wants us to know that as the giver of life, He is the only one who has the right to end it. To take matters into our own hands can be viewed as our willful intention to usurp God's authority—to figuratively shake our finger at Him and say, "It's my life, and I'll do with it what I want." If we trust God with our lives, then we must also trust Him when it is our time to die.

If you've read *A Teen's Guide to Christian Living: Practical Answers to Tough Questions About God and Faith*, perhaps you remember a beautiful and heartfelt story called "Wounded Angel" by eighteen-year-old Genta Tyla Murry. In the story a young woman named Laura was suicidal and considered ending her life. Luckily, she got help for her depression. Still, the greatest insight for her understanding that she must choose life over suicide didn't come only at the hands of her excellent therapists. Reading the Bible one evening, she came to understand that she didn't have a right to take her life. "I eagerly expect and hope that I will in no way be ashamed, but will have sufficient courage so that now as always Christ will be exalted in my body, whether by life or by death. For to me, to live is Christ and to die is gain. If I am to go on living in the body, this will mean fruitful labor for me. Yet what shall I choose? I do not know! I am torn between the two: I desire to depart and be with Christ, which is better by far; but it is more necessary for you that I remain in the body," she read in Philippians 1:20–24. Laura said these words "ministered to my crying soul" and helped her realize that taking her life was against God's Word—and so she vowed to God that she never would. After all, if she loved God—and loved those around her as God loved her—then she must choose to live. Scripture had shown Laura that "to live" must be her goal.

We might ask ourselves, *Why does God allow us to suffer in the first place?* God would have us know that for all of our circumstances—uncomfortable and seemingly intolerable as they appear—He allows us to feel burdened at times, even for our will to be tested: "The Lord examines the righteous" (Ps. 11:5). In James 1:3–4 we learn that it can even be for our own good: "The testing of your faith develops perseverance. Perseverance must finish its work so that you may be mature and complete, not lacking anything." From these words we learn that, although our lives look to be a mess, difficult and challenging times can be a necessary catalyst to get us to stop, take stock and regroup. Pain, heartache and sorrow cause us to mature, to deepen our faith and to grow closer to God. As I said in the introduction to my book, *A String of Pearls: Inspirational Stories Celebrating the Resiliency of the Human Spirit,* "While happiness feeds the heart, it is tribulation that opens the soul." Difficult times may cause us to question not only what we are doing, but why. Feeling at wits' end, even broken, can move us closer to God, and so we turn our eyes heavenward. Certainly, we are assured that God will not give us more than we can bear. "No temptation has seized you except what is common to man. And God is faithful; He will not let you be tempted beyond what you can bear. But, when you are tempted, He will also provide a way out so that you can stand up under it" (1 Cor. 10:13).

These are heavy thoughts, aren't they? But knowing what God expects is comforting. Don't feel you have to shoulder life alone: No one expects anyone to have all the answers. Should you be facing overwhelming problems or feel sadness and despair, be sure to talk to an adult you trust. Have a talk with your youth pastor as well. And don't forget to take your burdens to God. God knows about despair; he knows of the shame we hide; he knows when we have heavy burdens. God affirms that nothing is too great to bring to Him. He will bring us peace. He will restore us. He will make us whole and new. When we have sinned and can hardly bear our shame, when we need renewal and a fresh start, know that God will grant it. "I will repay you for the years the locusts have eaten" (Joel 2:25).

We only need to ask. "If we confess our sins, he is faithful and just and will forgive us our sins and purify us from all unrighteousness" (1 John 1:9).

God Expects Us to Love Our Enemy: Is He Serious?

Loving ourselves is one thing, but what about our enemies? "Love your enemies, do good to those who hate you, bless those who curse you, pray for those who mistreat you" Christ commands in Luke 6:27–28. Is he serious? What does God mean when he says that we must love our enemies? Surely He must know that, in some cases, this is most difficult to do!

Rest assured, He means it. Jesus said, "If you love those who love you, what credit is that to you? Even 'sinners' love those who love them. And if you do good to those who are good to you, what credit is that to you? Even 'sinners' do that. . . . But love your enemies, do good to them and lend to them without expecting to get anything back. Then your reward will be great, and you will be sons of the Most High. . . . Be merciful, just as your Father is merciful" (Luke 6:32–36). What God means here is that we should not let the way someone treats us affect the way we treat him in return. This idea completely wipes out any thoughts we have of getting revenge or getting even. We cannot control how someone else acts; we only can control how *we* act.

God also says that we should pray for our enemies—that we should pray for good things to happen to them. And here's even more good news! Amazing things happen when we begin to pray for our enemies; it changes us! It's really hard to nurse a grudge when you're praying for good things for someone. Why would Jesus suggest we bother loving our enemies? Because it is precisely the kind of love that mirrors the love God has for us. Nothing destroys our health, mars our countenance and robs our joy like hatred. It's the worst kind of illness. When we nurse anger, we are hurting ourselves. God would say for our own good to rise above it, act in a way we won't regret and move on.

Upholding God's Sixth Commandment— A Word from Your Peers

In the sixth Commandment, God asks us to not take the life of our fellow travelers. Because God models His love for us, we are likewise asked to model it for others. What does it mean to love our fellow human beings? It means that we are to help and befriend each other in their every need. We are to be our brother's keeper. How do we show God that we are grateful for our lives and respect the lives of His children everywhere? Here are some suggestions from your peers.

1. Don't be the cause of someone's death.

    I try to be a good driver and to watch out for myself when I drive. I don't want to kill someone because of my carelessness or because I couldn't avoid an accident due to someone else's carelessness. So that's one way I try to uphold this Commandment. Another way is that I've made a decision to abstain from sex for now. A good friend of mine got a girl preg-nant, and she had an abortion. It was heartbreaking for every-body—for the two of them and all the family and friends who knew about it. I'd be totally horrified if I caused someone to get pregnant, and the mother of the child might get an abortion. I'd have to answer to God on that, and I can't think of anything more terrifying. I know that to God, life is sacred; it is to me, too.

—Daniel Lathrop, 19

2. Obey the laws designed to protect us.

I drive as safely as I can, especially when I have others in the car with me. If I did something thoughtless and my recklessness caused a friend's death or caused him to be paralyzed for the rest of his life, I'd never forgive myself. I try to be very conscious about any way I may be a part of endangering someone else's life. I never drive "under the influence." I think that DUI (drinking under the influence) is like firing into a crowd with a loaded gun. I'd like to tell you that I never drink, but sometimes I do. But when I do drink, I never get behind the wheel of a car. And I make sure I never get into a car when the driver has had alcohol or used drugs.

—Larry Rogers, 17

3. Stop the hate in your home, school or community.

I think we must all do our part to rid the world of petty and nasty behavior because it snowballs into hatred. Where I work, there's a lot of gossip about various employees. I used to listen in, but I prided myself that I didn't pass along what I heard. But listening in gives others the idea that I want to hear gossip and that I value what I hear. Now when I come upon someone doing that, I either turn and walk away so they "get it" that I don't wish to be a part of it, or I make a point of saying something positive about that person so that it can, in some way, turn the negative feelings around. When I do this, there'll usually be this moment of uncomfortable silence, but then someone changes the subject, which is just what I intended.

Sometimes we look at the world and think, "What a violent world!" Then we turn around and are rude to someone or make them feel bad about themselves. I saw a lot of this in high school, and you know, it's a terrible thing we do to others. I agree that hate leads to violent acts. But we can, each one of us, work to change things. I'm working on doing my part.

—**MaryLynn Jones, 22**

4. Care enough to help others.

The other day I was riding to school with a friend. We pulled up to a stop sign, and there was a homeless person holding a "Will Work for Food" sign. My friend rolled down her window and gave him three dollars. When I remarked that her actions only encouraged that he beg for money rather than work, she replied, "He looked like he needed help, and I had some to give." Her comment, though said sweetly, stung. I was seeing the man out of disgust for "needing"; she was seeing him from the eyes of her willingness to be needed. And so she helped him out. I thought her actions were loving. In that moment, my heart got bigger. There is no shortage of opportunities to help out one another in the world today. Look around or ask around, and you will find that within a short distance there will be someone who needs something. But first, look inside yourself to see if you, like me, need an attitude adjustment.

—**Marissa Gonzales, 16**

5. Take care of your own spirit.

I think it's really important to do something when we see ourselves getting overwhelmed or depressed. God does not want us to get so despondent or depressed that we consider ending the pain. When that happens, we need to pray for guidance and peace for our own lives.

—**Jessie Marie Conley, 15**

6. Consider no person off-limits in sharing the good news of Jesus.

> *There are so many people who have fallen or lost their way. There are so many who need to be rescued by means of a loving, nonjudgmental voice of reason and counsel. Prisoners need support and encouragement to begin a new life. All such fellow humans need God's saving and sanctifying love. It is the privilege and responsibility of God's children to be His messengers of goodwill and brotherly help to those in need. In this way, we serve our Lord and Savior. "I was hungry and you gave me something to eat; I was thirsty and you gave me something to drink; I was a stranger and you invited me in; I needed clothes and you clothed me; I was sick and you looked after me; I was in prison, and you came to visit me. . . . Whatever you did for one of the least of these brothers of mine, you did for me" (Matt. 25:35–36, 40).*

> **—Ryan Phillips, 24**

7. Be a social activist.

> *Because business and politics are too often the instruments of injustice, it is the Christian's privilege and duty to take an active interest in the civic affairs of his community and country. Each of us must make sure that justice prevails, that security of life and home be guaranteed, and that each person has a right to earn his daily bread. When we do not take part or do our part when a need exists, when we fail to offer our full influence to make the lives of others better, then we sin against God. As God reminds us, "Anyone, then, who knows the good he ought to do and doesn't do it, sins" (James 4:17).*

> **—Jennifer Leigh Youngs, 28**

Keeping God's Commandment

Perhaps when you started this chapter you thought, *I could probably skip this chapter, because I've never murdered anyone!* But now that you see the broader implications of the Commandment, you've undoubtedly wondered if you need to have a heart-to-heart with God. If you feel there are some ways you've sinned against God, ask God for forgiveness. Then take positive steps to make amends. This may mean apologizing to someone you've wronged. It may mean changing habits—the way you act, the things you say. It may mean that you'll want to reach out to someone in need and make his life better.

Be big enough to reach out and lift up someone who is down. Do this because you love God. Do this because you have deepened your sense of responsibility and obligation to God's children. Always be thinking that you need to thank God for His love for you and then demonstrate the love of Christ to others.

YOUR PERSONAL JOURNAL

In what ways does God's sixth Commandment apply to your life today? In what ways is it still relevant?

_____

_____

_____

_____

_____

_____

_____

Think about your lifestyle. In what ways do you break the sixth Commandment?

_____

_____

_____

_____

_____

_____

_____

In what ways do you uphold God's sixth Commandment?

_____

_____

_____

_____

_____

_____

In the sixth Commandment we learn that we're not to cause hardship or suffering. What do you think this means for those at school or at your job who deliberately inflict pressure or in some way cause others to feel bad about themselves?

_____

_____

_____

_____

_____

Because each human life belongs to God, why wouldn't God have just made our lives easier so that the temptation for doing bad was something we never even thought about?

_____

_____

_____

_____

_____

_____

What is being done at your school or college to stop hate crimes? What else do you think needs to be done?

_____

_____

_____

_____

_____

_____

Do you think that some people are just naturally good, while others are born "bad apples"? Do you think that some people—such as "hardened criminals"—never can be rehabilitated? Explain.

_____

_____

_____

_____

_____

If someone is on death row, then accepts Jesus Christ into his or her life and now is "born again," would that be reason enough to take that person off death row? Explain.

_____

_____

_____

_____

_____

_____

_____

According to the sixth Commandment, can anyone—the presidents of countries included—justify taking the life of someone who has killed another? Explain.

_____

_____

_____

_____

_____

"Whoever sheds the blood of man, by man shall his blood be shed" (Gen. 9:6). What does this Scripture mean to you?

_____

_____

_____

_____

_____

_____

Because to God each life has eternal value, do we have an *obligation* to carry the message of God to the "ends of the Earth"? Explain.

_____

_____

_____

_____

_____

_____

In God's eyes, what is the difference between *murder* and *killing*? In what ways do you differentiate between them?

_____

_____

_____

_____

_____

_____

Within the context of war, is killing against God's sixth Commandment, or is it justified? Explain.

_____

_____

_____

_____

_____

_____

_____

Under the sixth Commandment, is a murderer only someone who kills intentionally, as in shooting someone to death, or is it also the person who causes someone to die in an accident in which he was driving recklessly or under the influence of drugs or alcohol? Explain.

_____

_____

_____

_____

_____

_____

God wants us to know that even neglecting to help others is a sin against His Commandment. In what ways have you been guilty of this? Give an example.

_____

_____

_____

_____

_____

God says, "Anyone who hates his brother is a murderer" (1 John 3:15). In what ways do you feel hate can lead to murder? Explain.

_____

_____

_____

_____

_____

_____

Do you think that the term "murderer" applies to someone who produces, sells or advertises cigarettes or liquor? What about those who promote things that destroy a person's spirit or desire to serve God? Is this a sin against this Commandment? Explain.

_____

_____

_____

_____

_____

_____

Do you feel that suicide is a sin? What if a person has an incurable disease or a terminal illness—might that be grounds for ending one's own suffering? Under the sixth Commandment, should people be imprisoned if they aid in an "assisted suicide"?

_____

_____

_____

_____

_____

_____

How is your life going? Are things fine or are you facing over-whelming problems or feeling sad and despondent? Who can you talk with about it? Have you had a heart-to-heart about this with God?

_____

_____

_____

_____

_____

_____

The Bible tells us that we must care for each other. In what ways do you carry this out?

_____

_____

_____

_____

_____

_____

Would you describe yourself as being your "brother's keeper"? Give an example of the last time you were.

_____

_____

_____

_____

_____

_____

The Bible tells us that it is our privilege and responsibility to be His messengers of goodwill and brotherly help to those in need. In what ways do you do this? Give an example.

_____

_____

_____

_____

_____

_____

Would you consider yourself a social activist? What do you do that demonstrates that you are? If you are not, what could you do to be an "instrument of justice" for others? Who would you most likely help out: young children, teens or senior citizens?

_____

_____

_____

_____

_____

_____

Do you believe it is a Christian's privilege and duty to take an active interest in the civic affairs of his community and country? In what ways do you see yourself doing this?

_____

_____

_____

_____

_____

_____

_____

Christ commands that we love our enemies. "Love your enemies, do good to those who hate you, bless those who curse you, pray for those who mistreat you" (Luke 6:27–28). What does this Scripture mean to you? Give an example of a time you've done this.

_____

_____

_____

_____

_____

_____

_____

Do you pray for your enemies? Why or why not? What would be the benefit of doing this?

_____

_____

_____

_____

_____

_____

_____

In what ways would the world be different if everyone upheld God's sixth Commandment?

_____

_____

_____

_____

_____

_____

_____

_____

In what ways would the world be different if *you* upheld God's sixth Commandment?

_____

_____

_____

_____

_____

_____

How can you keep from growing complacent about upholding God's sixth Commandment?

_____

_____

_____

_____

_____

_____

THE SEVENTH
COMMANDMENT

You shall not commit adultery.

Exod. 20:14

In the previous chapter, you learned that we each are God's creation and that, as such, our lives *belong* to God. Because each human life has eternal value to God, He decreed human life as sacred and warned that we were not to destroy the life of another. In fact, in His very comprehensive sixth law, God also commanded that we do no bodily harm nor cause any suffering. Instead, we are to help and befriend each other in every need.

In the seventh Commandment, God expands upon how we are to conduct ourselves in relationship to others, this time as it relates to sexuality. The seventh law explicitly commands that sexual intimacy be regarded as sacred—saved for marriage, privileged only for a husband and wife. In Genesis 2:18, we learn of the origin of God's sense of importance for the bond between a man and a woman: "It is not good for the man to be alone; I will make a helper suitable for him." God created man and woman to stand together, and so He joined them in marriage. Marriage, then, was a gift from God to us. God intended that marriage and family should be one of mankind's greatest joys on Earth, a foundation for true happiness.

As you already know, in each Commandment God guards something that is of the greatest importance to our welfare. What could be more basic to the welfare of a happy marriage than keeping it together? As always, there are consequences for all our actions, good or bad. God says this about anyone who should interfere with His intention that marriage be chaste and pure between a couple: "Marriage should be honored by all . . . for God will judge the adulterer and all the sexually immoral" (Heb. 13:4). Obeying this Commandment shows that we revere, love and trust God, and love our "neighbors" as God loves us.

Is God's Seventh Commandment Still Relevant Today?

"Pure and chaste": Does that sound old-fashioned, or what? How can this age-old Commandment possibly speak to our lives today?

It's understandable why God was concerned about the institution of marriage in times of old. It was by God's design that each man have only one wife (monogamy). But then polygamy (having two or more wives) came into existence (as a result of the falling away from God—a practice that Genesis 4:23 tells us started among the descendants of Cain). While Noah and his sons each had only one wife, polygamy crept in again, and at the time of Abraham it had become standard practice once more. God had to do something! And so His law was aimed at restoring marriage in the form He'd intended. At the time of Jesus, monogamy had been established among the Jews.

But that was then, and this is now. We all know that having children outside of marriage is not so good—with our busy lives and complicated lifestyles, kids are a lot of work for even two people (although in some 40 percent of homes, there are enough parents to go around—sometimes two and three sets of step-parents, even grandparents). And besides, we've heard the psychologists who have told us that it's best for children to have the influence of both male and female parents, which is why we're extra careful to practice safe sex in the first place. With that morality in place, what's so wrong with having sex as long as it's between two "consenting" adults? For one, there are those pesky—and risky—sexually transmitted diseases. And what about the inner lesions—the feelings of shame and guilt for those who offered up their bodies only to discover doing so meant little to the other party?

If God places an exclusive value on sex, how must He view those among us who rewrite the moral code to fit our own situation, to meet standards determined by our personal desires? Is this Commandment relevant in today's times? To find the answers, let's explore this "ancient" Commandment and see how it still speaks to you—a young adult living in new and promiscuous times.

Why Does God Ask Us to "Hold Out" on Sex?

When was the last time you said (or heard anyone else say), "I choose not to have sex until I'm married because I want to remain chaste and pure"? Few would say this for fear of having laughter break out, right? Unfortunately, many young adults are made to feel "prudish" if they wish to abstain from sex—to remain "chaste and pure." After all, in today's times, sex is commonplace—just an ordinary experience—in many relationships. Does that make it okay, then?

You are probably not marriage-minded right now (which is good). You may be in seventh grade, tenth grade, twelfth grade or college. Maybe your college years are behind you, and you are now in the workforce, or maybe you went to work full-time right out of high school. Whatever your circumstances, you probably are still pretty young to take on the responsibilities of marriage. Still, like most people, you're probably hoping one day you might "settle down." But for now, you're just looking forward to getting together with a special someone this weekend. Does this Commandment speak to you? Absolutely. And in a couple of ways.

Are You Having Sex?
God's Definition of Adultery

From the Commandment we learn what God has to say about premarital sex—an issue you'll confront sooner or later, if you haven't already. God calls sex outside of marriage "adultery."

God defines adultery as any and all sexual acts outside of marriage, saying that engaging in such acts are the same as cheating on one's spouse. If the notion of saving sex for marriage sounds old-fashioned and archaic to you, keep in mind that marriage always has been a primary concern for God. In fact, the marriage union is so esteemed by the Creator that He used the image of a bridegroom and his bride to describe the relationship between Christ and his church. And by the way, you may be interested in knowing that an entire book in the Bible (The Song of Solomon) is devoted to the beauty of married love. If you've not read this incredibly beautiful chapter, you'll want to! When you do, you'll discover young adults aren't the only ones who can write sizzling poems and letters about love!

And surely God knows that with sex comes a swarm of emotions. Entering into a sexual relationship places the focus on the physical aspects of a relationship—not the spiritual, social or other important opportunities for the couple to get to know each other. Promiscuous sex also exposes us to the very real possibilities (especially in today's times) of contracting venereal diseases or AIDS, or getting pregnant. God knows all this, of course, and would like to prevent His children from being hurt by experiencing "too much too soon." Even when we practice "safe sex," bringing sex into our relationships can leave us feeling cheated, "cheap," used and empty.

You're no doubt familiar with the *Taste Berries for Teens* series, a collection of books my daughter and I have coauthored for young adults. These books are filled with poignant, true-life accounts of young people who are making decisions about their lives in the most positive ways they can—by setting goals and doing all they can to put their dreams in motion. For some, doing this is a relatively simple matter of finding support and putting positive energy behind their goals. For others, it's a matter of starting over—of having to deal first with the consequences of having entered into experiences that were "too much too soon"—premarital sex being one of these.

God doesn't want us to get hurt, feel wounded, used or have experiences that are "too much, too soon." He wants us to feel whole, pure and chaste. The mandates of the seventh Commandment allow for a better chance of that. So by reserving sex for marriage, is God trying to keep something wonderful from us? Not at all. God wants us to enjoy his gift of physical intimacy to its fullest, but He knows the pain, guilt and chaos involved when misused. God just wants us to wait expectantly until the person He has ordained for us is truly ours.

You Don't Have to Play the "Sex Card"

Do you honor your Heavenly Father's seventh Commandment? If so, you aren't alone. Today, more and more young adults are upholding God's law and finding that doing so brings happiness—even relief from the pressures that accompany playing the "sex card." Seventeen-year-old Brad Weston shares his feelings on this.

> *I think that many teens feel they have to play the "sex card" in order to have a boyfriend or girlfriend. From what you see on TV to what you hear your friends tell you, it seems as if everyone is having sex. You begin to believe everyone is and that if you're not one of them, you're a geek. At my school, everyone talks about who is having sex with whom and who "puts out."*
>
> *The thing is, the sex thing is a joker card run wild: On the one hand, other teens expect you to be open-minded about it, but then if you openly discuss it, then you're considered "wild." If you aren't having sex or are talking against sex, then you're a prude. Even adults send conflicting signals. Most parents tell their kids not to engage in sex, but then give them the "safe-sex" lecture. And, of course, there's the blatant*

"it's okay" message staring at you in the student center: the condom dispenser. Everyone thinks everybody is having sex, which makes it seem "standard." If you ask me, when it comes to knowing what is black or white on this issue, I'd say that for a lot of young people today, the color has turned to gray. It's all pretty confusing.

I've been out with girls who force the issue: They expect sex to be a part of the date. Personally, I don't want to be expected to initiate sex with a girl I've asked out, nor do I feel it's right to bring the whole sexual thing into a relationship when I'm so young. I know it's where many teens take their relationships, but it doesn't make it right. Sex changes everything—it gets convoluted from that moment on.

I'm only seventeen, so for me, for now, it's enough just to have a special someone in my life. I like the idea that I can be myself and just have a good friend, someone with whom I can hold hands, walk to class, sit with at lunch, and talk with on the phone about school and things going on in my life. Just to have a person who is there for me and who thinks I'm cool is enough for now. I've talked to my friends who say that once they start having sex, their emotions are all over the place, and their relationships with family and friends change.

Personally, I think sex should be saved for marriage, and the girl I like thinks so, too. So all the pressure is off. And I especially like the idea that someone I like hasn't offered her body to anyone. I really respect that. She's not like this one girl in my class, who the moment she has a new boyfriend, she's laid him. What's that about, anyway? Then she wonders why no one respects her. Duh!

If we don't consider sex to be special—something that is meant to be shared with the love of our lifetime—then how can that be a good thing for our relationship with God? We've gotten so lax about sex that hardly anyone speaks up about it, so no wonder so many teens don't find sex to be any big deal.

When I enter into a sexual relationship with someone, I definitely want it to be a "big deal"—to me and to her.
—Brad Weston, 17

"Second-Time Virginity": You Can Restore Yourself in God's Eyes

As Brad so eloquently points out, you don't have to play the sex card. But what if you've lost your virginity and now regret that you didn't wait? Whether premarital sex was a choice you made or the result of date rape or incest, know that you can feel whole again. A healing release comes through forgiveness. This is important because unresolved guilt or pain kills our happiness, and can even make us sick or cause depression.

Forgiving ourselves is often the hardest type of absolution. This is another reason why reading Scripture is so important. The Bible is filled with accounts that help us understand our own situation and see that God is familiar with our plight. Do you remember when the Pharisees brought a woman to Jesus whom they had caught in the act of adultery? They wanted to stone her according to Jewish law, but Jesus knelt down on the ground and began to write in the sand. The Pharisees stood angrily, expecting to carry out a brutal execution. Instead, Jesus quietly said, "If any one of you is without sin, let him be the first to throw a stone at her." Because they then understood, the accusers began to drift away from the scene. When they had all gone, Jesus said to the woman, "Then neither do I condemn you. Go now and leave your life of sin" (John 8:7, 11). Isn't that beautiful? Jesus would say to you, too, "I don't condemn you for what you've done or for what has happened to you. Go now, but sin no more." God wants you to know it's never too late to turn your life around. As we learn in Joel 2:25, "I will repay you for the years the locusts have eaten."

How do you turn your life around? You begin by asking God to help you accept forgiveness for your own shortcomings. And you ask Him to help you forgive those who hurt you, just as God forgives them and you. Ask Him to help you to once again be "chaste and pure." He will forgive you and restore you "unto" Himself. As we are reminded in 1 John 1:9, "If we confess our sins, He is faithful and just and will forgive us our sins and purify us from all unrighteousness." You are His child. He is your Heavenly Father. God wants you to know that nothing you have done or experienced is too much for Him to forgive.

If you need to ask someone else to forgive you, don't put it off. The sooner the better. And ask God to help you make amends to anyone you have hurt. As He promises, "Be strong and courageous . . . for the Lord your God goes with you; he will never leave you nor forsake you" (Deut. 31:6).

Another good way to resolve some of the pain you may be feeling is to talk things over with your youth minister or parents. When you decide you want to stay sexually pure from this day forward, you can experience a second virginity. This second virginity comes by asking for God's forgiveness through Jesus and by committing to stay sexually abstinent until marriage. Reclaiming your purity can give you a whole new outlook and freedom in your life, or as we learn in 2 Corinthians 5:17, "If anyone is in Christ, he is a new creation; the old has gone, the new has come!"

You might also contact an organization called "What If . . ." that promotes second-time virginity or visit the Sex Respect Web site at *www.sexrespect.com/PromoteTeenAbstinence*.

Some people have a past they wish they could erase. A lot of times, we do things we wish we could take back. You may have been involved in premarital sexual activity and wish you could blot it out of your past and be rid of all the memories. Whatever may have happened or whatever your sin, God offers second chances! His forgiveness is a gift. Accept it.

God's Criteria for Finding the "Perfect" Relationship

Maybe you have a boy- or girlfriend, or maybe that's still a "to-be" for you. You never should feel pressured to be in a relationship, no matter what your age. Maybe you've decided to just focus on school, friends and sports for now, and that's really good, too. Maybe you're seventeen, eighteen, nineteen or in your early twenties and already are "promised" or even engaged to someone. Maybe you're "in love" and both of you feel this way about each other, even though you know this probably isn't the person you'll end up marrying. Or maybe it is; you've found your "one and only"—and are positive you are altar-bound.

How can you be sure this person is right for you? Again, the Bible provides answers. Looking out for our relationship happiness, God laid out a blueprint for the ideal marriage in His Word. Even though you aren't married, God's plan for happiness in married life contains some good advice for making even a dating relationship a godly experience.

What Does It Mean to Be "Equally Yoked"?

What would God want for us? For starters, He wants us to be "equally yoked." Interesting phrase, isn't it? What do you think it means? Scripture says, "Do not be yoked together with unbelievers. For what do righteousness and wickedness have in common? Or what fellowship can light have with darkness?" (2 Cor. 6:14). "Equally yoked" means that the two of you agree on some very important things, the very first being that God comes first in your lives. Consider how this would apply to your dating life. If both of you put God at the center of your lives, as a couple, would you be more likely to be "on the same page"? Would the two of you then be more likely to support each other in upholding God's laws? As it relates to God's seventh law, would "being on the same page" mean abstaining from premarital sex was a mutual value? Because both of you feel blessed by God's love, are you more likely to hold off on premarital sex?

What could be more important to a couple than to share the same love of God? What wonderful, common ground! Being equally yoked would be a tremendous joy and blessing for the two of you, as eighteen-year-old Chad Jarvie explains:

> *My faith in God defines who I am. I could never be with someone who isn't a Christian. I want someone who can share that important part of my life with me. I like asking a girl to go to church with me, and I especially like being asked by friends to go to church with them. When I ask someone out knowing she is God-centered, that's really attractive to me. That she believes in God means that I already know a great deal about her character—which is very important to me, as well. Of course, I'm not thinking of getting married anytime soon, but if I ever change my mind, it would be because the girl I'm with is someone who is a Christian. If she and I want to take our relationship to another level—even decide that someday we want to be married—then I'm assured that we have at least a chance of making a go of it. Because we're "equally yoked," we'll have talked about what church we both will attend and really discussed what sort of home life we both want. I know from looking at my parents' marriage that a family divided on such issues is headed for unhappiness and possible ruin. My parents come from different religious beliefs, and they mistakenly assumed that the other would convert. But after they got married, each discovered that the other person was unwilling to change. After I was born, they really fought: Mom wanted me brought up in her faith; Dad wanted me brought up in his. So I learned from experience that faith can bond you together or be the wedge that makes a happy home impossible. My parents divorced when I was nine. I'd like to create a home and*

keep it together, for always. My feeling is that if I start with being equally yoked, I'll have a better chance at that. If choosing a suitable mate is important to married life, then why wouldn't the same apply to dating life? It does for me.

—**Chad Jarvie, 18**

Chad makes a very important point about the importance of dating someone who shares your faith. My mother always used a phrase: "Be careful who you date: you may be choosing your mate." In my teen years, that didn't seem all that important to me, but I can see now that it really is. Choosing a "suitable" dating mate is more than finding someone who is kind, smart and attractive—although admiring these things about your sweetie is a good thing, too!

What Does It Mean to Be "Pure in Mind and Body"?

God would also like for us to be "pure in mind and body." It's not easy to dismiss sex with "Just Say No." From television to movies to the Internet, all seem to promote casual sex as just fine, even the thing to do. Maybe you feel that without "sex appeal," you'll be a nerd, a loner without a friend in the world or worse. And, of course, your hormones are raging, sending an "I want" message of their own. Perhaps your parents are giving you mixed messages, as in "I don't want you to have sex; if you do, use condoms." So what are they saying: "Abstain," or "Practice safe sex"? Unless you attend a Christian school, your teachers may be saying something similar. Maybe you believe premarital sex is fine if you practice "safe sex." From your family to health classes and sex-education programs, you're taught the facts about human reproduction, contraception and sexually transmitted diseases—so maybe you think having sex is okay as long as you take all the right precautions.

Commitments and values regarding premarital sex differ so widely in society that you're bound to be confused about where you stand on the issue. Can God's Commandment help point you in the right direction? The challenge for you is to not only make sense of the facts in order to make wise choices, but to run them by God as well. Where does God fit into the picture?

God wants us to learn to control our natural sex urges—and He offers help in doing so. He wants us to submit our lives to living close to Him. When we love Him—when we study His Word and come to Him in prayer—He watches over us so that temptations don't overcome us. "Watch and pray, so that you will not fall into temptation" (Matt. 26:41). If you ask Him, He will help you through the lure of playing the sex card—and the empty message of "sex is no big deal." Ask God to help you keep your mind pure by turning your heart away from pornography, illicit movies and sex magazines, and to help you keep your distance from those who take interest in such activities. God will help you stay "chaste and pure."

"You're Very Cute; Do You Believe in God?"

Hopefully, you have established some boundaries for intimacy in your relationships with the opposite sex. If not, it's time to do that. It's so easy to believe that you can keep your physical touching and romantic actions to a minimum, or you can just stop if things start to get out of hand. Those who are older and have been down that road know the real truth. It's hard to stop a runaway train, and sexual intimacy is like that. You may have succeeded once or twice, but it will become harder to continue holding back those feelings that are a natural part of your emotional and physical makeup. Those feelings are God-given and are not wrong, per se. They are just meant to be expressed freely in married relationships. You don't have to "prove" anything to a boyfriend or girlfriend, and you surely don't have to prove anything to other friends who may want to know how far you will go. Anyone who respects himself or herself will also respect you.

Be aware of your feelings. Date in accordance with your parents' or guardians' guidelines. You can use the old "safety in numbers" adage to your advantage and choose to go out in groups. Remember that "God is faithful; He will not let you be tempted beyond what you can bear. But when you are tempted, He will also provide a way out so that you can stand up under it" (1 Cor. 10:13). Ask God to help you with the temptations you're facing.

So what if you don't have a special someone in your life right now, but you're looking? Short of going up and saying, "You're very cute; do you believe in God?" what should you look for? Choose someone whose moral and spiritual values are those you admire and respect, someone who is kind and considerate, and treats his other friends and family with utmost respect. And don't forget to have a heart-to-heart with God. He hears your every prayer. He knows—even more than you do—what will make you happy. Make it your goal to share your time with only those who you know will make God happy.

God Knows What Makes Us Happy

You will almost surely fall in and out of love several times before you find the person who is right for you. When you make that commitment, it is intended to be for life. The Genesis story so beautifully tells of the first woman literally coming from man, "bone of my bones and flesh of my flesh . . . For this reason a man will leave his father and mother and be united to his wife, and they will become one flesh" (Gen. 2:23–24). Marriage is a sacred covenant, which is not usually what you see depicted on many television sitcoms or in movies today. As long as you and your partner are "equally yoked," meaning you share the same faith in God and enough similar interests, your relationship can be as blessed as God intended.

God's seventh Commandment is still necessary in today's times. The world might try to dismiss it, explain it away or tell us it's outdated, but it's not so. God knows what makes us happy; He knows what harms us spiritually, emotionally and physically. Misuse of sex can do all three. Maybe you know first-hand how adultery causes pain because your parents divorced after one was unfaithful to the other. Maybe you have experienced sex prematurely and have come to realize that, outside the context of marriage, it's not healthy. Remember Jesus' precious words, "Neither do I condemn you. Go and sin no more."

If you have upheld this Commandment, thank God and pray you will continue to remain pure. If you have stepped over the boundary, promise yourself and God that from this day forward you will uphold His seventh Commandment.

YOUR PERSONAL JOURNAL

In what ways does God's seventh Commandment apply to your life today? In what ways is it still relevant?

_____

_____

_____

_____

_____

Think about your lifestyle. In what ways do you break the seventh Commandment?

_____

_____

_____

_____

_____

_____

In what ways do you uphold the seventh Commandment?

_____

_____

_____

_____

_____

_____

The seventh Commandment explicitly says that sexual intimacy is to be regarded as sacred—saved for marriage, privileged only for a husband and wife. Do you consider your relationship with God to be so sacred, so special, that you'll uphold His Commandment? Explain.

_____

_____

_____

_____

_____

_____

What if you are "in love"? Is it okay to have premarital sex then? What if you wish to uphold God's Commandment, but your partner does not. How would you deal with that?

_____

_____

_____

_____

_____

_____

Do you and your friends discuss issues that pertain to sex, such as safe sex, the consequences of unprotected sex or saving sex for marriage? Do you discuss these issues in relationship to the seventh Commandment? Why or why not?

_____

_____

_____

_____

_____

_____

When was the last time you said to a friend, "I'm saving sex for marriage"? What was the reaction?

_____

_____

_____

_____

_____

_____

When was the last time a friend said to you, "I'm saving sex for marriage"? What was your reaction?

_____

_____

_____

_____

_____

_____

If everyone is talking about having sex, if it seems ordinary—does that make it okay, then? Explain.

_____

_____

_____

_____

_____

_____

In biblical times, God was pretty furious when His people sinned against His seventh law. What must God think about our blatantly ignoring the seventh Commandment in today's times? Explain.

_____

_____

_____

_____

_____

_____

God intended that marriage and family be one of mankind's greatest joys on Earth, a foundation for true happiness. Why, then, do you think 50 percent of marriages end in divorce?

_____

_____

_____

_____

_____

_____

If everyone upheld the seventh Commandment, do you think there would be fewer divorces? Explain.

_____

_____

_____

_____

_____

_____

The Song of Solomon is devoted to the beauty of love. If you haven't read it, do that now. How does the Book of Solomon "speak" to you?

_____

_____

_____

_____

_____

_____

God says that we are "to wait expectantly" for the person He has "ordained" for us. What does that mean to you? Do you believe God has someone special in mind for you to love for a lifetime?

_____

_____

_____

_____

_____

_____

Brad Weston said that many young people "play the sex card." Do you see that happening among your friends? Or, do you think young adults are upholding God's seventh law?

_____

_____

_____

_____

_____

_____

Have you lost your virginity? If so, do you regret that you didn't wait? Why or why not?

_____

_____

_____

_____

_____

If a good friend told you he or she was thinking about having premarital sex, what advice would you give that person? Do you think that person would value your advice? Would your advice also include that premarital sex goes against God's desire for keeping us "chaste and pure"?

_____

_____

_____

_____

_____

_____

Are you dealing with any serious sexuality issues right now, such as pregnancy, date rape or incest? If so, who have you spoken to about it? Have you talked to God about it? Do you think you need additional help and support in moving beyond the pain, guilt or shame you feel? Who can you turn to for help and support?

_____

_____

_____

_____

_____

If you've had premarital sex, do you believe God will forgive you and restore you to feel "chaste and pure"? Why do you feel this way?

_____

_____

_____

_____

_____

_____

If you've not had sex, how does this chapter support you in reserving sex for marriage? What was the single most persuasive argument you read to save sex for marriage?

_____

_____

_____

_____

_____

_____

Do you have a special someone in your life? Is upholding God's seventh Commandment important to that person? Do the two of you talk about it?

_____

_____

_____

_____

_____

_____

Have you ever been (or do you know friends who have been) pressured into having sex? Are you (or they) still seeing that person? Why or why not?

_____

_____

_____

_____

_____

_____

_____

_____

What's your plan for abstaining from premarital sex? If you've already had sexual relations, what's your plan for—as God asks of you—to "go and sin no more"?

_____

_____

_____

_____

_____

_____

What does being "equally yoked" mean to you?

_____

_____

_____

_____

_____

_____

Have you ever had a boy- or girlfriend who put God first in his or her life? What was that like? Did you feel that because of it, the two of you were both "on the same page"? Did it help you address issues such as how you should conduct yourself in the relationship? Explain.

_____

_____

_____

_____

_____

_____

If you don't have a special sweetie in your life right now, but you're "looking," short of going up and saying, "You're very cute; do you believe in God?" how will you know that person is a Christian? What are the qualities you'd like this person to have?

_____

_____

_____

_____

_____

_____

What does being "pure in mind and body" mean to you?

_____

_____

_____

_____

_____

_____

Do you feel that pornography contributes to adultery? Explain.

_____

_____

_____

_____

_____

_____

If you've already found your one and only true love, is it okay for you to have sex with this person? Explain.

_____

_____

_____

_____

_____

_____

_____

Do you trust God to bring the right person into your life? How will you know when that person has arrived?

_____

_____

_____

_____

_____

_____

_____

In what ways would the world be different if everyone upheld God's seventh Commandment?

_____

_____

_____

_____

_____

_____

_____

In what ways would the world be different if *you* upheld God's seventh Commandment?

_____

_____

_____

_____

_____

_____

How can you keep from growing complacent about upholding God's seventh Commandment?

_____

_____

_____

_____

_____

_____

_____

THE EIGHTH
COMMANDMENT

You shall not steal.

Exod. 20:15

I n the previous chapter, you learned the seventh Commandment explicitly commands that sexual intimacy be regarded as sacred—saved for marriage, privileged only for a husband and wife. Regardless of the ever-present temptations enticing our hormones, we're expected to save sex for marriage, and we're explicitly cautioned against leading others astray.

An up-close look at the eighth Commandment shows that it, too, governs personal conduct, but this time as it relates to the "property" of others. We are not to rob our fellow "travelers" of their belongings through unfair dealings, fraud or any other means.

As always, God is most sincere that we uphold His law: "[Neither] thieves nor the greedy nor drunkards nor slanderers nor swindlers will inherit the kingdom of God" (1 Cor. 6:10). Because we revere, love and trust God, and love our "neighbors" as God loves us, we uphold God's eighth Law.

Is God's Eighth Commandment Still Relevant Today?

As you reflect on this Commandment and assess its implications for your life, you may be thinking, *You know, this Commandment could very well apply to me.* As Baron Ruzgar admitted, "God's got me on this one: There was that candy bar I stole from my neighborhood grocery store when I was eleven and the Tommy Hilfiger cap I borrowed a few months ago from Mike Olaf that I didn't return because I really like it. I'm guilty for taking money on several occasions from Mom's wallet without asking. And just this past week I drove the family car without my dad's permission."

According to the eighth Commandment, do you think Baron is "guilty"? He is. Property is *anything* that belongs to someone else. In Baron's situation, not only did he "steal" from the proprietor of the grocery store, his classmate, Mike Olaf, and his family, but he took from God, as well. Anything and everything that belongs to us also belongs to God. God is the Creator, therefore He is the owner of all things: "The Earth is the Lord's and everything in it" we learn in 1 Corinthians 10:26. "'The silver is Mine and the gold is Mine,' declares the Lord Almighty" (Hag. 2:8).

It's not so difficult to see how Baron's taking the candy bar and the money qualify as "theft." But taking the family car without permission or the Tommy cap still hanging in his closet—did he "steal" these things, or do they fall under the category of deception? In the eyes of God, is there a difference? You be the judge. Let's look at God's intent in the eighth Commandment and see how it applies to our lives today.

How Does God Define "Property"?

As you know, in all His Commandments God guards something that is of great importance to our welfare. It's fairly easy to see how a Commandment of this nature could be important in days of old, a time when food was scarce and people were in dire need of water and food and other things just to survive. Perhaps it was common to steal a goat, sheep or other possessions. I grew up on a farm, and it was not at all uncommon to discover that a thief had made off in the night with several chickens, geese or farm tools. In ancient times, maybe other items such as a slingshot or handmade jewelry passed down from parent to child or brother to brother disappeared, perhaps to be sold or traded for other necessities. It's not difficult to figure out that mankind has always thieved from each other for one reason or another. And what a sad statement that is! Right now, as you read, someone is taking something that belongs to another, maybe in the room next to you. Do you or any of your brothers or sisters or friends download music or term papers from the Internet? With few exceptions, that would be stealing.

Does this ancient Commandment have anything to teach us in a time when it seems as though many people will do and say almost anything to get what they want from others? Is God's eighth law relevant in a world where seemingly everyone is looking out for only him- or herself? Can we use this law to guide our morality, not only to refrain from taking from others, but to appreciate and be satisfied with what we already have? How much do we need to be happy? If "less is more," can we appreciate and be content with less? Let's have a closer look at the love behind this very important Commandment.

Is Skipping Class (or Work), or Downloading Music from the Internet, Stealing?

There are many ways to take "property" from another. Stealing, robbing, cheating and deception are but a few. God says that even those who "cater to the weakness" in others are guilty of "stealing" (which is exactly what Baron did when he asked a classmate—who describes himself as "intimidated" by Baron— to "borrow" his cap, knowing he had little intention of ever returning it). Does this mean, then, that someone who sells merchandise known to be harmful—such as alcohol, cigarettes or illegal drugs—is breaking God's eighth Commandment? What about selling a "bogus" idea—such as purposefully deceiving someone so as to take advantage of his or her property? What about skipping class or calling in sick for school or work when you just want the day off? Certainly, taking the teacher's answer book is stealing, as is knowingly walking off with the pen at the bank-teller's window. What about downloading music from the

Internet, "loafing" on the job, or wasting your time and talents? Yes, all are transgressions against God's eighth Commandment.

How about you? Do you always uphold the Commandment? Think about that for a moment. In what ways might you be guilty of "stealing"? On page 219 in the journal section, make a list of the things you've done that God might consider stealing. In going over your list, were you surprised that it was as long (or short) as it was? Were you amazed by the things you included as "theft"? Let's take a closer look at God's list of "These are mine: Don't steal them from me."

What Belongs to God? His "These are Mine: Don't Steal Them from Me" Inventory

We transgress the eighth Commandment by withholding from God what is His. What, then, is God's? Maybe more than you think. It's a long list. For starters, our lives, time, talent, service and love all belong to God. If we discover that we've been guilty of stealing from God—even if it's unknowingly—what should we do? According to God's Word, "He who has been stealing must steal no longer" (Eph. 4:28).

Following is a partial list of God's "property"—and God's intent for the way we should use them while on our life's journey. As you'll discover, just as we must take utmost care not to damage something we've borrowed from someone, we must be just as careful with those things on loan to us from God.

1. *Our lives.* God created us. We are His children. Our lives belong to Him. Because we are all God's children, naturally we all belong to Him. He decides when we are born and when it is time for our souls to depart from their physical forms (death). Never is this more poignantly stated than in Isaiah 43:1: "I have summoned you by name; you are mine!"

   As inclusive as this is—that our very souls belong to God—

we are reminded that everything we "have" and all that we are about is God's, too. This includes our time and talents, the way we treat His children (our family and friends and neighbors)—everything! The land we buy (or hope to buy) on which to build a home, our children and our children's children, the material possession we acquire—from the jewels we unearth to the fruits of our labor—all belong to God. Whatever the number of years of life we are given, we are but stewards here on Earth. As we learn in 1 Timothy 6:7, "For we brought nothing into the world, and we can take nothing out of it."

2. *The purpose of our lives.* "For I know the plans I have for you," declares the Lord, "plans to prosper you . . . plans to give you hope and a future" (Jer. 29:11). God assures each and every one of us that He has a plan for us, and so there is a purpose to our lives—and God lays claim to it. Although God expects you to "desire" wanting to find it—you are to search for it—He lets you know when you've found it. If you doubt this, ask any born-again Christian if he or she has found his or her purpose. You'll discover that this person can articulate his or her purpose succinctly, and with a great deal of zest, zeal and delight.

Have you discovered your purpose in life? Finding it seems elusive and difficult at times, and feelings of being "empty" and "lost" are but the half of it. Solomon reminds us time and again in both the book of Proverbs and in Ecclesiastes how empty our lives can be when we focus on the wrong things. What really counts? At times when you feel maybe you haven't a clue as to what direction you should take, what sort of love, friends, career or work toward which you should be heading, have you considered that it might be God's plan that you feel a little "lost" searching on your own? God wants you to come to Him in prayer, asking Him if He'll guide you, direct you and let you know when you're on track. We shouldn't think we're to find our life's purpose on our own.

We are to ask God what He would have us do with our lives. "Teach me to do your will, for you are my God" we learn in Psalms 143:10. Have you talked to God about His intentions for your life? Have you asked God to give you insight and direction for finding your path, your work, or for simply making your way in life? He wants you to. God promises that He will put you in fertile soil where you will bloom, and that you will be like that tree planted by the water "which yields its fruit in season and whose leaf does not wither" (Ps. 1:3).

3. *The time we are given.* We are not to squander years waiting to "get a life." God gives each of us the same twenty-four hours in every day. Does God care how we spend ours? He does. At the end of time, we each will have to answer for how we spent our time on our earthly journey. It doesn't do much good to fret over someone else's life. Answering for our own is a big enough load to carry.

Have you thought about how you're going to honor God with the time He's given you? Are you using your time wisely? Have you asked Him if He's pleased with the way you're using yours? Certainly, He has much to say on this: "Sow your seed in the morning and at evening let not your hands be idle, for you do not know which will succeed, whether this or that, or whether both will do equally well. . . . So then banish anxiety from your heart and cast off the troubles of your body, for youth and vigor are meaningless" (Eccles. 11:6, 10).

How does God want you to spend your time in the future? When you think of "time," do your thoughts immediately turn to "work" or "job"? Maybe God wants you to spend your time caring for people—such as raising a family, or being in a job where you tend to others, such as being a therapist. Or maybe you're to work outdoors in nature, caring for the seeds of the Earth—such as being a gardener, a farmer or working in a greenhouse. Maybe He'll ask you to build a major corporation with branches and affiliates around the world that employs thousands of people. Maybe His plan is to have you write a book that will impact the world, changing the lives of millions—or maybe it will change just one—you. Or maybe you are to be the "love" in someone's life, the ray of light and joy that gives that person strength, hope and courage to go about his or her work, a work that is destined. Who is to know? God knows. "Seek first His kingdom and His righteousness and all these things will be given to you" (Matt. 6:33). Ask God to show you His plans that will lead you to living with purpose, and hence, acquire great joy and satisfaction.

4. *A tenth of all we earn.* We are to consider the practice of tithing as a holy act. Because everything we have ultimately comes from God, we're honored to tithe. Does God expect us to tithe? Yes, we are to give back to God a tenth of what we earn. "A tithe of everything from the land . . . belongs to the Lord; it is holy to the Lord. . . . Every tenth animal that passes under the shepherd's rod will be holy to the Lord" (Lev. 27:30, 32). In Genesis 28:22, we find Jacob, Abraham's grandson, pledging to God, "Of all that You give me, I will give You a tenth." And what if we skip this part of Christian living—is that okay? No. We are expected to tithe. In fact God considers that we are robbing from Him when we do not tithe, as we learn in Malachi 3:8: "Will a man rob God? Yet you rob Me. But you ask, 'How do we rob You?' In tithes and offerings" (Mal. 3:8).

God accepts more than just our money as a tithe. As an example, our "time" belongs to God, yet He gives us the free will to spend our time as we choose—although He did set aside Sundays for us to give back to Him. Our service to God or in the church is both a time and a talent tithe, then. Still, it's only one way we're to tithe. God's ultimate intention for our tithe is that it be used to further His Word to spread the message of Jesus. And by the way, God bestows blessings on those who tithe.

Does God expect us to be prosperous, then? While God does not speak to the standard of living to which we are to aspire, the eighth Commandment carries a warning about laziness ("slothfulness"). Laziness is covered many times in the book of Proverbs and elsewhere in the Bible. We are to *earn* our way. Not doing so is another form of theft. "If a man will not work, he shall not eat" (2 Thess. 3:10). We are to value work. Adam and Eve had work to do even before they totally goofed up the paradise plan (Gen. 2:15). God especially admonishes us to keep out of debt. "Let no debt remain outstanding except the continuing debt to love one another" (Rom. 13:8). We are to pay our way and to pay our debts. God expects us to be prudent, and to neither squander nor waste. "Gather the pieces that are left over. Let nothing be wasted" (John 6:12).

5. *Our fellowship (relationships) to others.* Because we are all God's "children," we naturally should desire to help one another. In Matthew 10:42, we learn about the simple art of sharing: You don't have to do more than give "even a cup of cold water" in Jesus' name to be of service. It pleases God to see us serving others and following the example that Jesus set for us when he walked the Earth. Not only is our "caretaking" of each other commanded, but doing so is good for our health and well-being. It's a well-known fact that one of the best prescriptions for feeling down is to help a person in need. Start by giving a happy heart and a joyous spirit to everyone you encounter in your day-to-day living—in school, on the job or in your neighborhood and community.

The gift of fellowship means that we are to look out for each other—to be our "brother's keeper." You can see the importance of this. A society where everyone looks out only for himself cannot create healthy communities. A society of selfish and self-centered people cannot grow thriving communities. A society of thieves cannot prosper. We must all commit to dealing fairly, to being honest, and to working for social conditions that make it possible for all to live in abundance in all the ways we can. "It is required that those who have been given a trust must prove faithful" (1 Cor. 4:2). Jesus Christ expects us to "serve" one another in love, as he did when he was among us. That means helping each other in all the ways we can. In this way we become the "salt (seasoning) and the light" of the world, demonstrating the love of Christ to others in need. We are directed to put the needs of others above our own, and to do this with great humility, just as Jesus demonstrated when he washed his disciples' feet. This is how much our Heavenly Father wants us to love one another. Again, to God, each human life is sacred. And so, God expects us to place this value on each and every soul, as well.

6. *Our strengths, gifts and talents.* Gifts and talents are those special abilities that we each are given. Sometimes we refer to these as "our strengths." Even though some people believe they have no special talent or gift, we each receive something. While for some this may be the gift of an outgoing and engaging personality, for another it may be the gift of a serene and peaceful nature. "To one there is given through the Spirit the message of wisdom, to another the message of knowledge by means of the same Spirit, to another faith . . . to another gifts of healing . . ." (1 Cor. 12:8–9). Yes, we've each been blessed with an attribute or strength that can be given back to God.

Our gifts, talents and special abilities are to be used in service to our "brothers and sisters" in the world. We're to reach out to others, to witness God's love and to share the Word of God. We're to serve those with whom we share our lives, and those whom God places in our path throughout the course of our lives. Why are we to do this? Because we hear God when He tells us that He wants us to love each other, as He so loves us. We are to do all we can to see to it that each hears the Word of God.

Why didn't God just give us all the same talents? These, too—our differences—are gifts from God. And so we each see and hear and learn things differently. What have you learned about yourself? Have you discovered, for example, that you best learn by hearing about something, or do you learn something more easily when you see it demonstrated? Maybe visual images best "speak" to you, or maybe it is through the power of music. These differences are much needed, as we learn in Ephesians 4:12–13. Blend your gifts together "so that the body of Christ may be built up until we all reach unity in the faith and in the knowledge of the Son of God and become mature." Are you to wait to use your skills until your retirement years when perhaps you'll have more time on your hands? No. You're to start now, as we learn in 1 Timothy 4:11: "Don't let anyone look down on you because you are young, but set an example for the believers in speech, in life, in love, in faith and in purity." He expects us to use our blessings. As we learn in James 2:20, "Faith without deeds is useless."

What if you don't know what your strengths are? It's a matter of looking closely and wanting to understand yourself. Once again, "mystery" is sometimes part of God's plan. He wants you to come to Him in prayer, to ask Him to help you discover your gifts, and to say, "Teach me to do your will, for you are my God" (Ps. 143:10). Have you done this yet?

Protecting God's Abundance

And so we learn that the eighth Commandment is not just about taking possessions from our neighbor. It is also about understanding what belongs to God. It's about being grateful for our lives and all that we have. It is about pulling our own weight, taking responsibility for the quality of our lives, while always remembering that we live in concert with others. We learn that the most grand of all goals we set and achieve is that we be "good and faithful servants" to our Heavenly Father, our Creator. We learn that tithing is to thank God for our abundance, so He will continue to bless us abundantly. It is about spreading the "Good News" to those with whom we share our time on Earth, as well as to those who come behind us.

By using the talents, gifts and nature of our personalities, we come to learn how each of us is needed—the different ways each of us is "called" to do God's work. We learn that no one is left out—not even a prisoner serving "time." He or she, too, has a role to play. In order to revere, love and trust God, and love our "neighbors" as God loves us, we must see that all our "brothers and sisters" are cared for, wherever they may call home on the planet. The apostle Paul writes, "We are God's fellow workers" (1 Cor. 3:9).

YOUR PERSONAL JOURNAL

In what ways does God's eighth Commandment apply to your life today? In what ways is it still relevant?

_____

_____

_____

_____

_____

_____

Think about your lifestyle. In what ways do you break the eighth Commandment?

_____

_____

_____

_____

_____

_____

In what ways do you uphold the eighth Commandment?

_____

_____

_____

_____

_____

_____

How does God define "property"?

_____

_____

_____

_____

_____

In God's eyes, what is "stealing"?

_____

_____

_____

_____

_____

_____

What is the difference between stealing and deception? In the eyes of God, is there a difference?

_____

_____

_____

_____

_____

_____

There are many ways to take "property" from another. Stealing, robbing, cheating and deception are but a few. To "cater to the weakness" in others is stealing, as well. Give an example of a time when you were guilty of doing this.

_____

_____

_____

_____

_____

_____

_____

Do you think that someone who sells merchandise known to be harmful—such as alcohol, cigarettes or illegal drugs—is breaking God's eighth Commandment? Explain.

_____

_____

_____

_____

_____

_____

Have you ever knowingly deceived someone? What did you do? Did you know at the time that what you were doing was sinning against God? If so, how did that make you feel about God and yourself?

_____

_____

_____

_____

_____

_____

In what ways are acts such as skipping class, downloading music from the Internet, loafing on the job, or wasting your time and talent considered stealing?

_____

_____

_____

_____

_____

According to God's Word, "He who has been stealing must steal no longer" (Eph. 4:28). What does this mean to you?

_____

_____

_____

_____

_____

_____

Have you ever knowingly "robbed" someone of his or her "property"? Do you think you will be able to return the item(s) you took? If not, in what way can you repay the debt, or is asking for their forgiveness (and God's) enough?

_____

_____

_____

_____

_____

_____

Write a letter to someone you stole from, apologizing for your actions.

_____

_____

_____

_____

_____

_____

How do you feel about all we have as belonging to God? Does that remove the burden of having to "keep up with the Joneses," or does it seem more like, "Then why bother acquiring land and all the other material possessions supposedly associated with living 'the good life'"? Explain.

_____

_____

_____

_____

_____

_____

What does this Scripture verse mean to you? "For we brought nothing into the world, and we can take nothing out of it" (1 Tim. 6:7).

_____

_____

_____

_____

_____

_____

Have you discovered your "purpose" in life? If so, what is it? If not, what do you think is holding you back? Have you talked to God about His intentions for your life? Have you asked God to give you insight and direction for finding your path, your work and your way in life? Why or why not?

_____

_____

_____

_____

_____

God cares about how we use our time. Are you using your time wisely? Have you asked God if He's pleased with the way you're using yours?

_____

_____

_____

_____

_____

_____

What does this Scripture verse mean to you? "Sow your seed in the morning and at evening let not your hands be idle, for you do not know which will succeed, whether this or that, or whether both will do equally well. . . . So then banish anxiety from your heart and cast off the troubles of your body, for youth and vigor are meaningless" (Eccles. 11:6, 10).

_____

_____

_____

_____

_____

Do you tithe one-tenth of all that you earn to God or the church? Why or why not? If you don't yet earn money, what else could you tithe to God that helps others hear His Word?

_____

_____

_____

_____

_____

In what ways do you serve others? In what ways do you feel you are making a difference in the world—at home, at school, in your community or for the planet?

_____

_____

_____

_____

_____

_____

Are you a Christian? If someone didn't know you personally, how would they know that you are?

_____

_____

_____

_____

_____

_____

What does this Scripture verse mean to you? "Teach me to do your will, for you are my God" (Ps. 143:10).

_____

_____

_____

_____

_____

_____

_____

The word "testimony" refers to a personal story of accepting Jesus Christ as Savior. What is your "testimony" story? When and where did you accept God into your life?

_____

_____

_____

_____

_____

What strengths, gifts and talents have been given to you by God? When did you discover—or uncover—this, and how did you know for sure? If you haven't as yet discovered them, what are your plans for stepping up your search? Do your plans include asking God for direction?

_____

_____

_____

_____

_____

God's Word admonishes us to keep out of debt. Why do you think that staying out of debt is important to God? What is your plan for doing this your whole life through?

_____

_____

_____

_____

_____

"Gather the pieces that are left over. Let nothing be wasted" (John 6:12). God expects us to be prudent, to not squander or waste. How does this Scripture "speak" to your life? How do you think it applies to conserving the Earth's resources?

_____

_____

_____

_____

_____

_____

Would you describe yourself as industrious, lazy or some-where in between? Explain. Why do you think that God dislikes "slothfulness"?

_____

_____

_____

_____

_____

_____

What does being your "brother's keeper" mean to you? In what ways have you recently acted as a "brother's keeper"?

_____

_____

_____

_____

_____

_____

We each have a part to play in spreading the "Good News." One way we do this is by going to church so as to "witness" that attending church and learning God's Word is important. Do you willingly attend church, or do you depend upon your parents to prod you into going?

_____

_____

_____

_____

_____

_____

_____

What do you think this Scripture means? "Do not let the sun go down while you are still angry" (Eph. 4:26).

_____

_____

_____

_____

_____

_____

_____

_____

In what ways would the world be different if everyone upheld God's eighth Commandment?

_____

_____

_____

_____

_____

In what ways would the world be different if *you* upheld God's eighth Commandment?

_____

_____

_____

_____

_____

How can you keep from growing complacent about upholding God's eighth Commandment?

_____

_____

_____

_____

_____

_____

~~State Property~~/God's Heir

Oh, Lord, what have I done with my life, and is it too late?
They say I'm not "me" but rather, "Property of the State."

Please tell me, Lord, how did I go so wrong,
And why is it that I keep hearing an angel's song?

Lord, am I forever forgotten or just temporarily lost?
Are there any answers and, if so, at what price: what is the cost?

I'm surrounded by endless miles of high, razor-sharp wire,
Living a regimented, tormented life; I'm soooooo unbelievably
   tired.

Locked behind a steel door in an eight-by-twelve cell,
I've done this to me! Now a creature living in hell.

Filled with feelings of worthlessness overpowered by fear,
Oh, sweet Jesus, tell me you love me; it's all I wish to hear.

It's been an agonizing life of suffering and way too much pain,
A life I've so trounced I've nothing to lose, but nothing to gain.

I've been so careless with me, shattered a once perfectly good
   heart,
Now I'm empty and hopeless; haven't a clue how to get a fresh
   start.

I look to You, Lord, to answer the questions within,
I look to You, Lord, to free me from the chains of great sin.

I ask Your forgiveness and to place a seed of love in my heart,
Teach me Your Will, rewrite my script; I cannot, will not, depart.

Hallelujah, Lord! I can make it now; I can feel You holding me
   close,
I love me now because of You, dear Lord, and I know it's at a
   time like this You love me the most.

I'm no longer just another number wasting away in this place,
I belong to the Lord—an heir, His heir—NOT "Property of the
   State"!

—**Casey Casto Ybanez, 17, a.k.a. #22445**

THE NINTH
COMMANDMENT

You shall not give false testimony against your neighbor.
                                    Exod. 20:16

B y now you've come to see that God *is* Lord, Master of the universe, a Creator who keeps a vigilant eye on all His creation, a possessive and loving Heavenly Father who wants custody of all His children—now and forevermore. The Almighty is a benevolent caretaker who stands guard as we go about our work and play, safeguarding us with the Commandments, ensuring that we treat those with whom we are sharing the journey lovingly and fairly. The house rules are simple and straightforward: We are to revere, love and trust in God, and love each other as He loves us.

As in all His Commandments, God guards something that is of the greatest importance to our welfare. In the eighth Commandment, God focused on theft. Because we all are His children, God rightly warned us that taking or stealing the "property" of another also was a theft against Him. In this chapter, the study of the ninth Commandment, God informs us that a "good name" is also an asset—one that is so highly prized, so valuable to each of us, that in no way are we to "steal it." We are not to tarnish, diminish or slander our neighbor's name. God is specific in what He means by this: We should not lie to, betray, slander or criticize our neighbor. As with many of the Commandments, God offers an extended portrayal of what we are to do. In this Commandment, God says of our neighbor that we are to "apologize for him, speak well of him and put the most 'charitable construction'" on all he or she does.

Our Heavenly Father is serious about our understanding and abiding by His law: "A good name is more desirable than great riches" (Prov. 22:1). Because we revere, love and trust God, and love our "neighbors" as God loves us, we consider it our honor, as much as it is our obligation, to hold our neighbor's name and reputation in the highest regard, knowing how important it is to his or her welfare.

Is God's Ninth Commandment Still Relevant Today?

In days of old, much like now, a person's reputation was most important. Whether accurate or not, others judge us—and hence treat us—according to our reputation. One can only speculate how this played out in biblical days, although surely if one had a reputation for being less than upright, it wasn't like you could hire a team of forensic specialists to see you through an ordeal. A reputation could work in your favor, as well, such as in the Good Samaritan story found in Luke 10:30–37.

Whether you're called a thief or a Good Samaritan, your reputation walks into the room before you do. And so God rightly warns us that we are not to go around "dissing" others. We're to make sure that any negative connotation associated with someone's name not be of our own doing, nor a by-product of words we let roll off our tongues. We're to speak only of the good we know about others, and, in fact, we're charged with putting the most "charitable construction'" on all that our neighbor does. Who does God consider to be our neighbor, and what does God consider to be a violation of His "giving false testimony" law? Let's examine the Commandment and see how it applies to our lives today.

Who Is Our "Neighbor"?

Silly question? Not really. Yes, it is the people who live in the house next door to you, of course, but in a larger sense, it includes others. For starters, it includes everyone with whom you come in contact on a daily basis. Who else might be your "neighbor"? Take a moment to list everyone who you think could be included as your "neighbor" on page 250.

Who is on your list? Does it include the members of your family, your friends and the students at the school or college you attend (including those you don't know very well or not at all)? Does it include teachers and support staff, such as the custodians, aides and secretaries? Does your list include the counselor, the school nurse, your principal and anyone else who makes the school day happen—from the administrators to the clerks who sort the mail? If you hold a job, does your list include any and all with whom you work? What about the people you encounter at the mall; at the library; the person who takes the tickets at the movies; the waiters and waitresses at your favorite restaurants or fast-food places; and the people you meet as you walk down a street within your community? Did you list police officers; firemen; the teller at the bank; any and all merchants within your community; and the homeless in your town? Did your list include anyone outside of your community, such as relatives living out of state—perhaps grandparents, aunts and uncles, cousins, nephews and nieces? Did your list include "neighbors" you do not know—such as the leaders from other countries as well as its citizens, from those living in elegant homes to those in the slums? Who else was on your list?

Was your list very, very long—or did you simply write down, "Every person in the world is my neighbor"? If you did the latter, you'd be correct. You see, there is no one in the world who is not your neighbor. As you would suspect, God's ninth Commandment applies to all His people. From the members of your family to your closest friends, from far-off countries to the Internet chat rooms, all are your "neighbors."

What Does "Giving False Testimony" Mean?

What does it mean to *give false testimony against your neighbor*? God doesn't mince words: We should not lie to, betray, slander or criticize our neighbor. We are responsible to God for the ways we uphold—or corrupt—the good name of others. Words, we learn, are *deeds.* "Do not let any unwholesome talk come out of your mouths, but only what is helpful for building others up according to their needs, that it may benefit those who listen" (Eph. 4:29). We are not to use our words to inflict hurt, pain or embarrassment upon anyone. Nor are we to use words that are meant to deceive, disparage or diminish the joyous and happy nature of our neighbor. The adage, "Sticks and stones may break my bones, but words will never hurt me," is not true. Words carried on the wings of love can soothe, heal, bring joy and possibility, while words riding the waves of anger leave destruction, pain, heartache and despair in their wake.

Giving false testimony results in loss. Damaging one's good name has ramifications, such as a tarnished reputation. We must not do this to our neighbor, but instead, guard our neighbor's name: "Each of you must put off falsehood and speak truthfully to his neighbor, for we are all members of one body" (Eph. 4:25). What should we do if we hear someone else uttering false testimony against our neighbor? God is clear in His direction: We should speak up, apologize for him and put the most charitable construction (to speak well of) on all that he is. We are to follow the example of Christ, who even when crucified put a charitable construction on this vile act of His enemies. He said, "Father, forgive them, for they know not what they are doing" (Luke 23:34).

The Value of a "Good Name"

What, then, we might ask, is the worth of a good name—and how destructive is a poor reputation? God leaves little doubt as to the importance of our "good name." The Bible tells us *a good name is part of our daily bread.* Certainly a good reputation has to do with making our way in life, whether it be to gain friendship or earn a living. Everyday experiences tell us people are unwilling to employ a person who has a reputation for being dishonest or unreliable. On the other hand, many are chosen for positions of trust and responsibility purely on their reputations for honesty and dependability, as sixteen-year-old Holly Stinson, who works part-time at a department store, found out.

> *A girl in my department had been with the company longer than any of the other full-time employees, so she was in line for a promotion to assistant manager. Still, she didn't get the job. It was given instead to a girl with the least amount of time on the job, all because everyone spoke well of her, always saying how impeccably honest she was and what a wonderful way she had with customers. Everyone knows that it was her reputation as a "wonderful employee" that won her the job.*
>
> **—Holly Stinson, 16**

Twenty-year-old Josh Anderson tells of an incident he recognized as giving false testimony.

> *My mom is a registered nurse in an emergency clinic at a local hospital. The clinic had wanted to hire a particular doctor from Houston, Texas—that is, until someone said they'd heard through the grapevine that he possibly had falsified information to insurance companies to get bigger payments. Learning of this, the hospital administrators changed their minds about the Houston doctor and hired someone else. In the end, it was discovered that no one had any proof that these allegations against him were real; no formal charges had ever been brought against him. No matter, the rumor completely obliterated this guy's chances of landing the job.*
>
> **—Josh Anderson, 20**

How about you? Surely you've seen the worth of a good reputation in your role as a student. A lot of grading is subjective, and teachers tend to give the benefit of the doubt to students known for their commitment to their studies. On the other hand, students with a reputation for not being "serious," or those who have been caught downloading papers from the Internet or cheating on their assignments may find it affects their grades. Robbie Carlton, seventeen, recalls such an incident that happened to him, one that created a great deal of stress.

> *Chemistry is my toughest subject, and I really have to work at it. So once, when there was a really big test, I took the time to study for it. As a result, I did really well on it. When I shared how well I had done with a classmate, he didn't believe I'd earned the grade. In an offhanded sort of way, he told my chemistry teacher that he was "pretty sure" I'd cheated. The teacher called me in and had me take the test over. Because I knew the material, I passed it, too. But it upset me that I had to. I did not cheat at all; I was simply prepared for the test. But the rumor changed my former "good" reputation with the teacher. From then on, she moved me to the front of the room on test days, presumably to keep an eye on me so as to be sure I wasn't cheating. Of course, being singled out and asked to take a seat up front was viewed with more than suspicion by my classmates. Some were curious and asked why the teacher was moving me, and others just giggled, as though they already knew. It was most demeaning. And I could tell that I lost enormous favor with the teacher. I never felt the "benefit of the doubt" from her from that time forward.*
> —**Robbie Carlton, 17**

Four Ways We Give False Testimony— A Word from Your Peers

Holly, Josh and Robbie know firsthand the value of a reputation. As their comments reveal, regardless of the ways in which we go about it, eroding the name of another creates loss in one way or another. Whether it be loss of a position, reputation, opportunity or income, if we cause (or contribute to) loss, it is an act of wrongdoing in God's eyes. While the "false testimony" Holly, Josh and Robbie talked about was relatively blatant, we also can bring about the demise of someone's good name in subtle ways, such as in the spirit or tone of what we say. There are many ways we can give false testimony against our neighbor, including these four "biggies":

Lie—make false statements
Betray—reveal secrets or private and personal information
Slander—make malicious comments
Criticize—diminish a person's stature in the eyes of another

And so we must be vigilant. Knowing how these "play out" can help us be on guard that we do not contribute to diminishing or ruining our neighbor's name. Here, then, is a word from your peers on how giving false testimony may be subtle, but is still wrong.

1. *To lie.* We give false testimony when we make statements about someone that are not true. Whether we do this to protect ourselves or someone else, or feel that doing so is a way to better our situation (or someone else's), all are most displeasing to God. Sixteen-year-old Cheerie VanCleef gives an example of a time when she lied about her friend for her own gain, and how it affected the lives of three people.

> *My girlfriend and I were doing research at the public library for a big paper that was coming due for a class. We were working away when a really cool guy walked by. My friend and I both noticed him at the same time, and then we discovered that he was staring at both of us. It was funny, and we all laughed. Then, glancing at the stack of research books piled in front of us, he broke the ice by saying, "Looks like you'll be here for some time!"*

We all chatted for a couple of minutes, exchanging where we each went to school and sharing a little of the projects we were working on. I was really taken with him, and I think my friend recognized this because when the guy left to return to his table, she said, "He's cute, and I think he likes you. You should go talk to him."

So I did, but just when I started thinking he was leading up to getting my phone number, he asked me for my friend's number! Turns out, the guy wasn't interested in me; he was interested in my friend. So I told him my friend had a boyfriend (so as to cut her out of the picture). When he asked how serious she was about the guy, I lied again, saying, "She's very serious about him." Well, nothing could be further from the truth. There was no guy in the picture; my friend had never even been out on a date!

The lies I told seemed innocent enough—at least in the beginning. But they led to all sorts of hardships. From that day forward, even though I wanted to ask my friend to come to the library to study with me or to help me do a paper (she's a real brain), I couldn't. I was petrified that we'd run into the same guy, and he'd find out that I was a liar. And then my friend would find out that I'd lied, and that would put a real strain on our friendship, maybe even end it. And because I was still hoping to run into the guy again, I went to the library every chance I got, hoping to see him again—but I couldn't take her with me. So that meant that when my girlfriend would call and ask me to hang out with her at the mall or go to the movies or something, because I'd want to be at the library (without her!) I'd make up a lie and tell her my parents had made some plans for me. Then I had to make sure that she didn't run into my parents—which was doubly hard because her parents and my parents know each other, and always run into each other at the cleaners or the grocery store. Talk about painting myself into a corner—it was miserable! One lie after another.

Sometimes even I had trouble keeping them all straight. It was tiring. It was an awful time. After a while, I wished I'd just let the two of them get together, because it wasn't like he was chasing after me! Telling lies, I discovered, is a lot of work. And that was before my conscience started bothering me!

Inside my head things got so confusing and so wacky. Finally, it got so bad that I just turned it over to God and basically said, "Okay, God, you've seen the mess I've made of this, and I'm in a corner. Can you please help me find my way out?" He did. He led me to see that I needed to level with my friend and ask her to forgive me, so I did. At first she was upset, but when I apologized and asked her to please forgive me, she accepted my apology, and then we laughed about it. She and I started going to the library again, and because that guy was hoping to run into my girlfriend again, he came to the library often and the two of them did get together. Of course, I had to level with him, too, and that was embarrassing! Anyway, the two of them have been going steady now for nearly four months. They're a great couple and really enjoy each other's company. He's become a friend of mine, too. God was good to me. So it was a lesson about not lying—and about God's forgiveness, as well.

—Cheerie VanCleef, 16

Twelve-year-old Robbie Wentzel learned that giving false testimony goes further than telling an outright lie.

If you don't speak up when someone is falsely accused, that's wrong, too. A kid at my school accused Alain of stealing money out of his backpack, but I knew Alain didn't take it—because I knew who did, and it wasn't Alain. But I didn't speak up and defend Alain, and that wasn't right. Because I didn't, his reputation as a thief remained—and I contributed to that. I still feel bad about it because I get upset when I'm accused of things that I don't do. So God must be really disappointed when we do these things to each other.

—Robbie Wentzel, 12

2. *To betray.* Revealing the secrets of another or disclosing private and personal information is another way we give false testimony against our neighbor. All can result in the loss of a "good name," as fifteen-year-old Larissa Linn knows because she did this to a teammate and saw how it all played out.

> *I play on the softball team at my school. Once, when the game was a long ways away, I stayed overnight at Cheryl Saxon's house. Other than being in my grade and playing on the softball team, we don't hang around together or anything. I stayed overnight with her because her mother was one of the drivers for Saturday's game, and it made things more convenient for everyone.*
>
> *Because of the early game, we went to bed around ten o'clock. Right around that time, her parents had a really big argument and started yelling at each other. I found that really uncomfortable—sometimes my parents yell at each other, but it sounds really awful when you hear it from people you don't know. Anyway, the next day, I told a couple of the girls on our team about it. I didn't necessarily do it to be malicious. I said something like, "I'm dead tired because I stayed with Cheryl last night, and her parents had a knock-down-drag-out-fight and I couldn't get to sleep after that."*
>
> *No one said anything to Cheryl about it at the game, but the next week, the incident was relayed to some other kids at school. Pretty soon, practically everyone knew. Unfortunately, every time someone told the story, it got bigger and sounded worse than it really was. By the time it got back to Cheryl, the word was that her parents were getting a divorce! Cheryl was totally humiliated. Cheryl's parents are really big supporters of*

the school, and, of course, her mom is one of the main parent volunteer drivers for the girl's softball team.

So what I said about her parents had a really terrible effect. Cheryl had invited me to her house for my convenience, and I had showed my appreciation by causing all this grief and tarnishing her and her family's "good name." I am really sorry, first because what I did was wrong, and also because I'd never want anyone to think my parents were as "terrible" or as unhappy with each other as everyone made Cheryl's out to be. Nor would I want anyone to think that my home life was "dysfunctional"—a word so many used when retelling the incident. It was really awful. I am so sorry to have betrayed her in this way. It was not fair of me at all. As a result of all this, I really watch what I say, how I say it, and why I say it.

—Larissa Linn, 15

Larissa understands better the importance of giving false testimony. Hopefully her classmates will understand their transgression in this incident, as well. When we pass along information about someone—be it gossip, hearsay, or information that may be true but has little or no positive value for building up another—then we are guilty of giving false testimony.

3. *To slander.* Slander is another way we give false testimony against one another. When we make malicious comments about someone, such as spreading gossip, or even when we pass along information knowing it's going to hurt or diminish the name of someone (even though it may be true), then we are sinning against God's ninth Commandment. Eighteen-year-old Steve Schachtenberger tells of a time he (falsely) manipulated the feelings of someone for his own selfish intentions.

I once told a girl I loved her so that she'd go out with me. I didn't love her; I was only trying to get her to like me so that I'd get the chance to have sex with her. Eventually, she began to like me, and we went out. Well, she refused to even make out with me, so I never asked her out again.

Then she found out that I'd asked her out for that one reason. She was really mad at me for that, but worse, she was really hurt. And then word got back to her that I'd told all my friends that we did have sex. That was so totally demeaning to her. I know because the counselor called me in and told me the girl was "devastated"—which is probably true because when she and some of her friends confronted me about what I had said and done, all she could do was stand there and cry. That made me feel pretty bad.

I do know that what I did was awfully mean, and I know it caused her a lot of heartache—especially when all the rumors about her having had sex went around school. While she isn't the sort of girl who most people would think of as having sex, I know it took a lot to quiet the rumor mill. Just from the guys' locker room, I can tell you that she was the butt of some pretty nasty jokes, and some pretty horrible things were written about her on the bathroom walls. Thinking back, I am sorry for my actions. I know what I did was wrong. I'm not very proud of myself.

—Steve Schachtenberger, 18

4. *To criticize.* Do you know anyone who is always finding fault with someone? You know the type: No one is ever "perfect" enough for that person. Always being critical, finding fault and being ungrateful are more than personality problems and character flaws. It's going against what our Heavenly Father wants for us. It's a transgression against His ninth Commandment, His law for the ways we are to treat each other—and to feel about each other. Why is criticism wrong in God's eyes? We might ask the question in this way, "What is the importance of speaking well of each other?" Let's take a closer look at this.

To help each other feel hope, to see possibility, to feel inspired to do what is good and best and right helps each of us to move toward taste-berry ideals. A "taste berry" is a little fruit that, when eaten, mysteriously convinces the taste buds that all food—even food that is distasteful—is delicious! This bright little berry has been used around the world for countless years to make tolerable the sometimes necessary eating of bitter foods, such as roots. In our *Taste Berries for Teens* series, my daughter and I use the taste berry as a metaphor. Has someone reached out when you were suffering a disappointment, nursing a broken heart or feeling overwhelmed? If so, that person was acting as your "taste berry."

As my daughter and I discovered in the *Taste Berries for Teens* series, when we help others by sweetening life's joys and easing the bitterness of its disappointments and losses—by helping them to see our world as full of hope, less impossible and more glorious—we inspire and motivate them to be more caring, helping and loving people. If we let them know that we will be there to help them out, whatever their situation or station in life, then we can change the world just by changing that one person's life. That is what God wants for us. We are to be our brother's keeper. It is our obligation—as much as it is our honor—to help others on a daily basis to see their lives in the most positive light.

On some days we all could use a taste berry, and no one knows this better than teens coping with the ups and downs of life. Taste-berry thinking allows us to apologize for our neighbor, speak well of him or her and put the most "charitable construction" on all that he or she does. Certainly no one likes to be around someone who is in the habit of always diminishing others, as fifteen-year-old Brad Forrest discovered.

> *I'm not exactly sure when it started, but I got into the habit of "dissing" others. It really didn't matter who it was. I was just down on that person. One day, while a group was*

gathered in the hall, I came sashaying up. Suddenly, the group disbanded. I was like, "Hey, where are you all going?" Almost in unison, everyone replied, "Away from you." That definitely hurt, so I learned that others don't really like to be around naysayers.

—Brad Forrest, 15

What if you don't actually say anything critical, but you're just listening to it? If you're feeling superior or pleased about someone else being "dissed," and thankful it's them and not you, are you are giving false testimony? Thirteen-year-old Tammy Metzler says "yes."

I used to hear people "slamming" others, and I was all ears. But then it dawned on me that if I'm getting satisfaction by hearing something bad about another person, what does that say about me? Now if it happens and I catch it, I will say something to neutralize the negative remark. From now on, I'm trying to think about what God wants before I let my tongue loose.

—Tammy Metzler, 13

If an Attorney Defends Someone Who Is Guilty, Is He or She Breaking the Ninth Commandment?

All of the above examples involve choices each teen made to break God's ninth Commandment. But what if it turns out to be the nature of your work—such as that of a defense attorney defending someone who is guilty? What would you do if you were in a situation in which you felt you had to tell a lie because something terrible might happen if you didn't? Galen Lenz's brother sometimes finds himself in this position. As Galen reports:

My brother is an attorney. He says in his profession, it's really hard to be representing someone, believing that person is innocent, and then finding out he or she is not. As that person's advocate, he has the responsibility to represent that person, so then he has to build a case for that person's innocence, knowing he or she is not. If he knows before he's taken on a person as a client that the person is guilty and looking for someone to get him off, then my brother won't take the case.

—Galen Lenz

What do you think—is Galen's brother guilty in the eyes of God? It makes for a good discussion, doesn't it? You might want to ask your parents, friends and youth pastor to talk this over with you.

Speaking God's Truths

Especially when we're young, it can seem like having the "scoop" on someone, to bring information to the table, can make you feel like you're "in the know." Always, it seems, people are willing to "get the goods" on someone—certainly our tabloids make us think so. Guard against thinking that you gain favor and power with others in this way.

Giving false testimony against anyone not only hurts that person, but tarnishes our own reputation, as well. If you are the sort of person who is the bringer of the "juicy news," then others will see you as a person who is all too happy to diss others. This reputation will be a mark on your own good character and set you up as someone who cannot be trusted. If someone talks poorly of another, do you think ill-spoken words about you are far behind? And what if you are not the person who is in the habit of treating others so poorly? You might look to Scripture to get up the courage to alert someone about the "wrong" they are doing, or make the decision to leave this so-called friend behind.

As we learn in 1 Corinthians 15:33, "Bad company corrupts good character."

Aside from letting each other down when we make it our business to put a mark on someone's name, an even bigger transgression is going on: We are expressly going against the Commandment that God has given us for how we are to revere, love and trust him, and love each other as He so loves us.

Start today by ensuring that everything you say and do honors the good name of others. It's important for them and for you—and it's important to God.

YOUR PERSONAL JOURNAL

In what ways does God's ninth Commandment apply to your life today? In what ways is it still relevant?

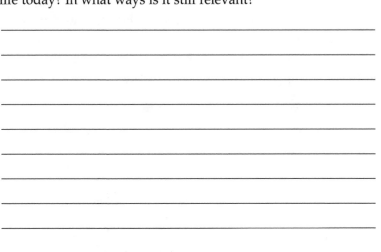

Think about your lifestyle. In what ways do you break the ninth Commandment?

_____

_____

_____

_____

_____

_____

In what ways do you uphold the ninth Commandment?

_____

_____

_____

_____

_____

_____

The ninth Commandment says we must not destroy the "good name" of another. What if a person already has an awful reputation—as a thief for example—and the reputation is deserved. (The person actually *is* a thief.) How does the Commandment apply then? Is it okay to share with others that you know this person to be a thief? Explain.

_____

_____

_____

_____

_____

_____

_____

_____

In what ways do you work to safeguard your good name with others? Is this something you regularly work at, or only when you think your good name is in jeopardy?

_____

_____

_____

_____

_____

_____

Give an example of a time when your good name was "jeopardized" and what you did to "salvage" it.

_____

_____

_____

_____

_____

_____

What do you do when someone is trying to demean you? Do you let it play out so the person can see for him- or herself that what he or she is saying or doing is not true? Or do you go to that person and tell him or her yourself? Or do you pray about it, asking God to make things right?

_____

_____

_____

_____

_____

Do you think it's important to safeguard "God's reputation"? In what ways do you do this?

_____

_____

_____

_____

_____

_____

Who is your "neighbor"? List everyone you can think of.

_____

_____

_____

_____

_____

_____

"A good name is more desirable than great riches" (Prov. 22:1). What does this Scripture mean to you?

_____

_____

_____

_____

_____

_____

In your life specifically, what does it means to *give false testimony against one's neighbor?*

_____

_____

_____

_____

_____

_____

This ninth Commandment says we are not to lie about, betray, slander nor criticize others. The next time you find yourself hearing gossip, do you think you will speak out? What might you say? How do you think those around you will respond to your doing this?

_____

_____

_____

_____

_____

_____

Why do you think people tell lies about others? Have you ever done this? Why?

_____

_____

_____

_____

_____

_____

_____

If you are in the habit of lying when doing so suits you, what have you learned about yourself that might lead you to understand why you do this? What are willing to do to refrain from being a liar?

_____

_____

_____

_____

_____

_____

Do you believe that words, like actions, are *deeds*? Explain.

_____

_____

_____

_____

_____

_____

"Do not let any unwholesome talk come out of your mouths, but only what is helpful for building others up according to their needs, that it may benefit those who listen" (Eph. 4:29). What does this Scripture mean to you?

_____

_____

_____

_____

_____

_____

Do you believe the adage, "Sticks and stones may break my bones, but words will never hurt me"? Explain.

_____

_____

_____

_____

_____

_____

We are told not to use words that deceive, disparage, disrupt or diminish the joyous and happy nature of our neighbor. What do you think this means? Give an example of how it applies to you.

_____

_____

_____

_____

_____

_____

Words carried on the wings of love can soothe, heal, bring joy and possibility—while words riding the waves of anger leave in their wake, destruction, pain, heartache and despair. What do you think this means? Who is the person you would most like to share these words with?

_____

_____

_____

_____

_____

_____

_____

Giving false testimony leaves a mark on one's good name. This, in turn, can result in a loss of reputation, which can then result in being deprived of an opportunity. Give an example of when this has happened to you.

_____

_____

_____

_____

_____

_____

What does this Scripture mean to you? "Bad company corrupts good character" (1 Cor. 15:33).

_____

_____

_____

_____

_____

_____

_____

_____

God leaves little doubt as to the importance of our "good name." What is the value of your "good name"? Have you ever lost your good name? What did you have to do to earn it back?

_____

_____

_____

_____

_____

_____

The Bible tells us a good name is part of our daily bread. What do you think this means?

_____

_____

_____

_____

_____

_____

_____

Give an example of a time when you were guilty of diminishing someone's good name through each of the following. What did you do to make things right? If you haven't, is it too late to do something? What do you think would be the best way to go about making amends if you haven't already done so?

A lie I told about someone:

_____

_____

_____

_____

_____

_____

Amends I made (or will make):

_____

_____

_____

_____

_____

_____

How I betrayed someone:

_____

_____

_____

_____

_____

_____

_____

_____

Amends I made (or will make):

_____

_____

_____

_____

_____

_____

A slanderous comment I made:

_____

_____

_____

_____

_____

_____

Amends I made (or will make):

_____

_____

_____

_____

_____

_____

I diminished the stature of _____ in the
eyes of _____ by _____

_____

_____

_____

_____

_____

_____

_____

Amends I made (or will make):

_____

_____

_____

_____

_____

_____

_____

_____

If you give false testimony against another, you tarnish your
good name as well. Give an example of a time when this
happened to you.

_____

_____

_____

_____

_____

_____

_____

_____

_____

A "taste berry" is a little fruit that, when eaten, mysteriously convinces the taste buds that all food—even food that is distasteful—is delicious. In what ways have you been a taste berry to someone? Who was that person? What did you do? How did your actions make that person's life "sweeter"?

_____

_____

_____

_____

_____

_____

_____

In what ways would the world be different if everyone upheld God's ninth Commandment?

_____

_____

_____

_____

_____

_____

_____

In what ways would the world be different if *you* upheld God's ninth Commandment?

_____

_____

_____

_____

_____

_____

_____

_____

_____

How can you keep from growing complacent about upholding God's ninth Commandment?

_____

_____

_____

_____

_____

_____

_____

_____

_____

_____

THE TENTH
COMMANDMENT

You shall not covet your neighbor″s house. You shall not covet your neighbor′s wife, or his manservant or maidservant, his ox or donkey, or anything that belongs to your neighbor.

Exod. 20:17

In the previous chapter, you learned how God considers our "good name" so valuable to each of us that He commands us not to slander, tarnish or diminish a person's reputation in any way. Not only are we not to "smear" anyone, but we're to be a "taste berry" to all we meet: We're to see each other in the most positive light we can. The Bible says we're to put the most "charitable construction" on all a person does. We need to ask ourselves why we would consider it our business to do a "takeover" on someone's name—certainly a person's own words and actions can speak for themselves. If we put a mark on someone's name due to having a mean spirit, jealousy or some reason we think is justified, it's not a good thing—and we'll have to answer to God for all we say and do.

The tenth Commandment is about a "takeover" as well, this time as it relates to "coveting" that which belongs to another. "Coveting" refers not only to taking someone's possessions, but to even being desirous (jealous) of things that belong to another. The first part of the tenth Commandment deals with real estate; the second portion deals with relationships and personal property.

As in all the Commandments, God guards something that is most important to our welfare. That we not contribute in any way toward anyone losing his or her possessions—be it that person's real estate or personal belongings, or the loyalty of that person's friends or other liaisons and associations—is certainly important to the well-being of all. Upholding the tenth Commandment shows that we revere, love and trust God, and love our neighbors as God loves us. As always, there are consequences should we not observe God's Word: "Watch out! Be on your guard against all kinds of greed; a man's life does not consist in the abundance of his possessions" (Luke 12:15).

Is God's Tenth Commandment Still Relevant Today?

It's not so difficult to see why a law commanding that someone not run off with your donkey or ox or wife (in the days of Moses, even a man's wife was considered his property) was necessary in biblical times. All were vital to day-to-day existence. But that was then, and this is now. You probably don't own a donkey or ox, or even want to. You know you can't afford a mortgage just yet, and besides, maybe you don't even like the style or location of your neighbor's house. And though your neighbor may have a wife or a husband, you're quite certain you're not looking for either just yet. As for coveting your neighbor's servants, well, you're not even sure if the neighbors have household help—and besides you know how to bake a pizza and you don't even want your parents to enter your room. So how can this antiquated Commandment possibly have meaning for you, a young adult living in new times? Think about that for a moment.

How does God's tenth Commandment apply to your life? Are you able to make a connection between the tenth law and the jacket you "permanently borrowed" from a friend or the Guess jeans one of your friends "borrowed" from you? Did you recall a newscaster telling of someone being robbed at gunpoint over a pair of Nike shoes or some other name brand? Did you find yourself wondering whether the tenth Commandment applies to things such as the media hype that says, "You, too, can be a perfect 10—if only you buy this product or that product!"?

The tenth Commandment has much to say about such things.

While you may not want an ox or a donkey, transportation is still very much an "item." Have you ever watched as someone got out of a "to-die-for" car and wished it were in your possession? Did you ever sometimes wish you *were* the person who possessed such beautiful wheels (or other things)? Or maybe you wished you had his or her job or lifestyle (or parents) so as to be able to afford such expensive things. Have you ever coveted anything? While you may not desire someone's spouse, maybe you sometimes look at your friend's boy- or girlfriend and wish that person had "feelings" for you rather than your friend. Or you may be desirous of someone's clothes, jewelry, cell phone or other gadgets. If you ever wished a certain friend's parents were yours, or that you could be a certain movie star or maybe even just the most popular person at school, college or where you work, than you'll want to consider how any or all are viewed in light of the tenth Commandment.

Let's take a look at how this ancient law applies to you, a young adult living in a materialistic world.

What Does It Mean to "Covet"?

The tenth Commandment definitely speaks to us regarding our "wished we had" list. Coveting—desiring that which belongs to someone else, even to the point of wanting to obtain it—is an easy thing to do when we're very young. As children, we sometimes coveted our friends' toys, even to the point of reaching out and taking them, and crying when we were told to give them back. It's natural for children to want to take whatever they want at the moment. But as we mature, we come to realize that such behavior is no longer acceptable, and, in fact, it is wrong to take that which belongs to another.

Why Is Coveting So Dangerous?

One reason coveting is so dangerous is because of where it can lead. When people desire the possessions of others, they may dream up a scheme to get them, steal them outright or even resort to underhanded means, such as murder, to possess them for themselves. Another reason we are not to covet the possessions of others is because such feelings can take over our hearts, separating us from God, as well as put a wedge between us and our neighbors, which you'll see is a common theme in the next section. God wants us each to earn our own way and to be grateful for what we have so as not to be consumed with desire for what others have. And yes, there is a difference between coveting and the longing for improvement and progress. The wish to improve oneself through work, study and industriousness are Christlike principles. This mind-set and work ethic go hand-in-hand with assisting and serving our neighbor.

This whole ideal is so important, so valuable, that God guards it by asking that we each look within. We each are to examine our heart to see that our motives are as pure as they can be. Your life—and all the things that you acquire—are about the abundance between you and God. God wants us to know that we can overcome temptation by asking Him to forgive us of our transgressions and to help us not to be tempted in the first place.

Coming to Terms with Greed, Envy and Jealousy—A Word from Your Peers

At this stage in life, no doubt you're setting goals and "going for it!" It's a time when you're looking to move forward in life, a time when you want to be as much like others as you can. Everyone wants to be accepted and fit in. And yet, it is this very mind-set that can tempt us into saying or doing almost anything to achieve that. In the following accounts, you'll read about young adults who tell of a time they coveted something and came to recognize it as such—be it envy over a friend's girl-friend, or someone's talent, intelligence or possession. Here are some of the ways young people say today's world make it "almost natural" to "covet"—and how they ask God to help them change their ways.

About three months into our school year, a new girl transferred to our school from out of state. The minute I saw Penny Hill, I fell madly in love. Three days later, I saw my friend, Jeremy, standing at his locker talking to Penny. As it turned out, she was instantly goo-goo over him. I was so jealous of my friend that I started bad-mouthing him to Penny every chance I got. And if he screwed up at football practice or didn't make a certain play, I'd let her know what a goof-up he had been. I'd belittle him or make him the butt of jokes right in front of her, as often as I could.

But Penny was so taken with Jeremy that she didn't care about any football flubs. Of course, it's also possible that she saw right through what I was doing, maybe even thinking I was a jerk. I say this because there was a time she'd listen to my words, then smile sweetly—as if my words were nothing more than words—and then turn her adoring attention to Jeremy. But as time went on, if she saw Jeremy with me, she wouldn't come up to us; she'd wait for when she could be with him when I wasn't around. It was plain to see that she didn't especially like my company—or the way I put down "her honey," as she called him. So that pretty much ended my hang-ing around with Jeremy, and worse, it put a dead halt to my being able to be anywhere near Penny. Still, it was really diffi-cult to get her off my mind.

Finally, I asked God to help me quit being obsessive over her. Jeremy and I aren't friends anymore because I think he felt I was trying to make time with Penny, and because I used a lot of excuses to be anywhere she was. Geez, jealousy sure can

*ruin things. I lost a dear friend, and even if Jeremy and Penny
break up, there is no way she'll ever give me the time of day.*

—Jonathan Morgan, 16

*My best friend, Julie Green, and I both wanted to own a car
so badly. In tenth and eleventh grades, it was at the top of our
wish list, something we talked about all the time. Neither of us
could afford one—not even an older used one. Nor could our
parents afford to help us out. Although we did get part-time
jobs, we carried a heavy load of classes and neither of us could
work many hours, which made saving for a car a near impos-
sibility. Then, on her seventeenth birthday, Julie's grandparents bought a new car and gave her theirs.*

*The car was black and looked almost new. She took the
money she had saved for a car and bought new rims and tinted
the windows. By the time she was done decking it out, it was
a beautiful car. I was so jealous that I would make snide
remarks about her having "rich relatives" (which wasn't the
case at all). At times, I was so rude to her that my behavior put
a strain on our relationship, but Julie was more than patient
with me. She was so happy that she had transportation and
because we were good friends, she just naturally assumed I'd
go everywhere with her. I did, of course, but in all honesty I
remained jealous of her and wished that her good luck had been
my own.*

*I remained envious for a long time—most of our senior year,
to be exact. I finally asked God to help me stop feeling jealous
and simply be happy for my friend. I'm nineteen now and in my
first year of junior college. I still don't have a car, but I no longer
envy others for the things they have. I try to just stay in a
"grateful" frame of mind; doing this makes all the difference in
the world. I feel like a better friend, and I am optimistic that I
will bring the things I want into my life through honest means.*

—Joanie Fulton, 19

A classmate of mine, Connie Conley, is a totally gifted artist. I consider myself talented, too, but I am nowhere near as gifted as Connie. I always thought of Connie's achievements as the level of talent I wanted to acquire. But it wasn't until a recent incident that I began to realize what a very destructive emotion envy is. The Chamber of Commerce in our town sponsored a contest for "Best Budding Artist." I entered it, of course. I wanted to win the $100 prize, along with a chance to have my art entered in the citywide competition (which awarded a $500 prize!).

When I found out about this contest through the local paper, I was hoping that maybe Connie wouldn't see it—or that if she did, it would be too late for her to enter. But she learned about it in plenty of time and talked openly about the drawing she was hoping to enter. Keep in mind that throughout all this, she encouraged me to enter; yet never once did I return her good-will. She wanted to win, too, but it didn't stop her from hoping for the best for me, her friend. The feeling wasn't mutual: I was not only hoping to win, but hoping she wouldn't. In fact, I was trying to think of any way to prevent her from entering. Every time I was at her house, I'd ask her to see her drawing—and even tried to think how I might spill a drink on it or in some way destroy the drawing. My envy ran so deep that I never once brought up anything about my having entered. Well, when the paper published the names of the winner and three runners-up, Connie had won first place! I was so upset! To be exact, I was less upset about my losing than the fact that Connie had won.

My feelings about her having won were really dark, and I knew it wasn't a good thing. Eventually I prayed about it, asking God not so much to make me a better artist (although I did ask for that, too!), but to help me get over my envy of Connie's remarkable talent. I probably don't have to tell you that the way I'd handled things caused a huge rift in my relationship with my friend. She thought it was strange of me to have never mentioned I'd entered the contest—especially since she'd been so open with me about her involvement and had shown me her drawing and all. It also probably didn't help that my drawing was a lot like hers!

We're still friends—barely—but certainly not as close as we once were. So I've lost on a lot of levels. For one, I didn't present a good entry. Because I always had my sights on Connie's work, I didn't really even tap into my creative self; my final submission was nowhere up to my best work. And then there was my "chill" with Connie, and I can't imagine that God was any happier either. I do know that to envy the talents and gifts of others goes against the way God wants us to care about others, and I am sorry I behaved the way I did. But I know that God has me in check now. I'm ready to simply admire the talents of others—and to feel grateful for my own.

—Jerelyn Smith, 17

I work twenty hours a week at a clothing store. We get a basic pay per hour, plus commission. I work really hard at helping customers find the things they like because the better my sales, the more my commission check. One of the other salespeople, Rachel, rings up a sale on her register number anytime she can get away with it—even though someone else works for the sale. A couple of Saturdays ago, a client came back to purchase some clothes she'd put on hold until she could decide if she really wanted them for sure. "They're being held for me by Mrs. Wilson," the client said. It was Mrs. Wilson's day off, so Rachel rung up the merchandise as being her own!

After the client left, I confronted Rachel and told her the sale did not belong to her, but rather to Mrs. Wilson. "She always makes great commissions," Rachel snapped. "Like she needs more! Have you seen the jewelry that woman wears? She must be a millionaire. Look, she doesn't need the commission like I do, so why should you care? Besides, I'm sick of her always making the best sales just because she's popular with customers." Clearly, Rachel was jealous. I told her that, regardless, the sale still belonged to Mrs. Wilson, and she had to make things right. Because I didn't have the confidence that Rachel would actually do that, I also informed the floor manager about what had happened. I think this is the real importance of asking God to walk with you in your life. I can see that Rachel works hard and needs all the commission money she can make. But it has to be acquired through honest means. Abiding by the Ten Commandments can help us do what's right—even when no one else is looking.

—**Brandy Perou, 17**

The Abundance of God
Shows Up in His Commandments

As you can see in the accounts by your peers, greed, envy and jealousy only serve to detract us from our best intentions; derail us from healthy and straightforward relationships with family, friends and others; and keep us mired in a pettiness that consumes us, keeping us from all that is good and best about our own lives. Moreover, dwelling in the pits of such destructive emotions separates us from God.

God wants us to be grateful for what we have in our lives so we won't be consumed with desire for what others have. This whole ideal is so important, so valuable, that God guards it by asking for each to look within. We each are to examine our hearts, to see that our motives are as pure as they can be. Your life—and all the things that you acquire—are about the abundance between you and God. Have you taken recent inventory of all you have? Have you thanked God for all He has given you?

When we really look at our lives, we realize that we have so much. Decide to live your life as simply as you can. Ask God to guide you, and guard you, in your daily life. Ask Him to help you see the bigger picture—to help you understand the purpose of your life—which is to come to know God and have a personal relationship with Him. This will help you see your life as full, abundantly full. As we are reminded in Luke 12:15, "Watch out! Be on your guard against all kinds of greed; a man's life does not consist in the abundance of his possessions." There is only one thing that is worth "coveting" and that is our relationship with God: "Show me your ways, O Lord, teach me your paths; guide me in your truth and teach me, for you are God my Savior, and my hope is in you all day long" (Ps. 25:4–5).

YOUR PERSONAL JOURNAL

In what ways does God's tenth Commandment apply to your life today? In what ways is it still relevant?

Think about your lifestyle. In what ways do you break the tenth Commandment?

_____

_____

_____

_____

_____

_____

In what ways do you uphold the tenth Commandment?

_____

_____

_____

_____

_____

_____

"Coveting" refers to not only taking others' possessions, but even to being jealous of things that belong to another. Write about a recent time in which you did that. What were you jealous about? How are things now?

_____

_____

_____

_____

_____

_____

_____

Have you ever coveted another person's possessions? What other things did you covet? Did you know at the time that you were "coveting"?

_____

_____

_____

_____

_____

_____

_____

How can God help you get over jealousy and envy? Have you ever asked God to help you do this? What happened then?

_____

_____

_____

_____

_____

_____

How would you explain to someone that it's wrong to covet someone else's possessions?

_____

_____

_____

_____

_____

_____

"Watch out! Be on your guard against all kinds of greed; a man's life does not consist in the abundance of his possessions" (Luke 12:15). What does this Scripture verse mean to you?

_____

_____

_____

_____

_____

_____

Have you ever had an "I-wished-I-was-like-so-and-so" or "had-the-things-that-so-and-so-has" list? Do you still have an "I-wished-I-had" list? What is on your list?

_____

_____

_____

_____

_____

_____

What does it mean to "covet"? Why is coveting so dangerous? Where can it lead?

_____

_____

_____

_____

_____

_____

_____

Have you ever "schemed" to steal or do something underhanded as a means to "possess" something that wasn't yours? What did you want? How did you go about getting it? How did you feel about yourself once you "possessed" it? Did you consider that your actions were transgressing against God and His tenth Commandment?

_____

_____

_____

_____

_____

_____

Another reason we are not to covet the possessions of another is that such feelings can take over our hearts, separating us from God, as well as put a wedge between us and our neighbors. How was that true for you in the situation you just wrote about?

_____

_____

_____

_____

_____

_____

Do you need to make amends to someone (or to God) for being covetous? If so, write a letter to the person asking him or her to forgive you.

Dear _____,

_____

_____

_____

_____

_____

God wants us to be grateful for what we have so we are not consumed with desire for what others have. How do you remind yourself to be grateful for what you have?

_____

_____

_____

_____

_____

_____

_____

In the tenth Commandment, God asks us to examine our hearts to see that our motives are as pure as they can be. How often do you examine your motives for wanting something? How do you keep your heart pure?

_____

_____

_____

_____

_____

_____

_____

What is the difference between "coveting" and "wishing for improvement and progress"? Why does God approve of improving oneself through work, study and industriousness?

_____

_____

_____

_____

_____

_____

How does the mind-set (work ethic) of working toward "improvement and progress" go hand in hand with assisting and serving our neighbor?

_____

_____

_____

_____

_____

_____

You are to love others as God loves you, but not covet anything of theirs. Your life—and all the things that you acquire—is about the abundance between you and God. What does this statement mean to you?

_____

_____

_____

_____

_____

In what ways would the world be different if everyone upheld God's tenth Commandment?

_____

_____

_____

_____

_____

_____

_____

In what ways would the world be different if *you* upheld God's tenth Commandment?

_____

_____

_____

_____

_____

_____

How can you keep from growing complacent about upholding God's tenth Commandment?

_____

_____

_____

_____

_____

Appendix A

Abbreviations for Books of the Bible

(Note: Books not commonly abbreviated are not listed.)

Old Testament

1 Chronicles	1 Chron.	Lamentations	Lam.
2 Chronicles	2 Chron.	Leviticus	Lev.
Daniel	Dan.	Malachi	Mal.
Deuteronomy	Deut.	Nehemiah	Neh.
Ecclesiastes	Eccles.	Numbers	Num.
Exodus	Exod.	Obadiah	Obad.
Ezekiel	Ezek.	Proverbs	Prov.
Genesis	Gen.	Psalms	Ps.
Haggai	Hag.	1 Samuel	1 Sam.
Habakkuk	Hab.	2 Samuel	2 Sam.
Isaiah	Isa.	Song of	Song
Jeremiah	Jer.	Solomon	of Sol.
Joshua	Josh.	Zechariah	Zech.
Judges	Judg.	Zephaniah	Zeph.

New Testament

Colossians	Col.	Philemon	Philem.
1 Corinthians	1 Cor.	Philippians	Phil.
2 Corinthians	2 Cor.	Revelation	Rev.
Ephesians	Eph.	Romans	Rom.
Galatians	Gal.	1 Thessalonians	1 Thess.
Hebrews	Heb.	2 Thessalonians	2 Thess.
Matthew	Matt.	1 Timothy	1 Tim.
1 Peter	1 Pet.	2 Timothy	2 Tim.

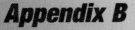

Appendix B

God's Ten Commandments
(Exod. 20:1–17)

1. I am the Lord your God. . . . You shall have no other gods before me.

2. You shall not make for yourself an idol in the form of anything in heaven above or on the Earth beneath or in the waters below. . . .

3. You shall not misuse the name of the Lord your God, for the Lord will not hold anyone guiltless who misuses his name.

4. Remember the Sabbath day by keeping it holy. . . .

5. Honor your father and your mother so that you may live long in the land the Lord your God is giving you.

6. You shall not murder.

7. You shall not commit adultery.

8. You shall not steal.

9. You shall not give false testimony against your neighbor.

10. You shall not covet your neighbor's house. You shall not covet your neighbor's wife, or his manservant or maidservant, his ox or donkey, or anything that belongs to your neighbor.

Appendix C

Simple Prayers for Christian Living

The Lord's Prayer

Our Father who art in heaven,
Hallowed be thy name;
Thy kingdom come.
Thy will be done on Earth
as it is in heaven.
Give us this day our daily bread.
And forgive us our debts,
As we forgive our debtors.
And lead us not into temptation,
But deliver us from evil:
For thine is the kingdom,
and the power, and the glory, forever. Amen.

The Serenity Prayer

God grant me the serenity
to accept the things I cannot change,
courage to change the things I can
and the wisdom to know the difference.

A Prayer for Salvation

Dear Father, I realize that I am a sinner
And that I cannot change anything I have done.
But You can give me a new life, Lord,
if I give my old one to You.
Forgive me for my sins and accept me into Your holy family.
I know that You sent Your only son, Jesus,
into the world to die for my sins. I believe that he is
the way, the truth and the life,
and I accept him now as my personal Savior.
Thank You, Lord, for hearing my prayer
and for giving me eternal life.

A Prayer of Thanksgiving

Heavenly Father, I offer You praise and thanks
for who You are and for all that You have done.
You have created this wondrous universe
and all things are under Your control.
You made me, Father, just the way You wanted me,
and You put in me your Holy Spirit
so that I could be more like You.
Your blessings are too numerous to count.
You have always been there with what I need
just when I need it.
I know I can bring any problem, no matter how small, to You
and You will help me work it out according to Your will.
I promise to love and serve You all of my life
because You want what is best for me.
May I always seek You first, above all else.

A Prayer for Healing

Dear God, today I am in need of Your healing touch.
You know just what ails me, even before I speak it.
You understand all that I am feeling because
You have suffered all things in the form of Jesus Christ.
Take my pain, Lord, and use it to show me Your truth.
If it is Your will, heal me and remove my pain.
If You have some purpose for this affliction,
Show me what it is, Lord.
"I can do all things through Him who gives me strength."
If You wish to make me stronger through this pain, Lord,
then so be it.
Give me the courage to withstand it
and the grace to be an example to others.
Forgive me if I sin in my pain and selfishness.
Show me that all things are working for good through You.

A Prayer for Courage

Father, today I need Your strength
to help me get through the challenges I am facing.
I know that You have not given me a spirit of fear,
but of courage and a sound mind.
Yet, I am frightened when I think of what I must do.
Strengthen me, Lord, and help me to shed my fear.
You are the God who delivered Daniel from the lion's den,
And I know You can deliver me if You choose to.
Father, show me how to stand tall
and to be bold in the midst of this situation.
Help me to do whatever I must to bring glory
and honor to Your name.
If you choose not to deliver me, then stand beside me
and help me to get through this.
Thank you, God, for being my help and my strength.

A Prayer for Peace

God, as I look around me I see people absorbed in conflicts.
The world is in turmoil because too many people
do not know You.
Open their eyes, Lord, and show them that You have the answer.
Send your Holy Spirit to convict and change hearts.
Only then will people understand what is truly important.
Father, help me to do my part in sharing Your truth
with others who do not know You.
Give me courage and wisdom
to know how to set a godly example for others around me to see.
As we all long for peace in the world, Father,
so we also long for peace in our hearts.
Touch the hearts of those who are suffering and oppressed,
Especially help those who are too weak to help themselves.
And, Father, give us the grace to forgive the oppressors.
You sent Your Son into the world to be the Prince of Peace.
May the world know that peace.

A Prayer for Grace

Dear God, You know what I am facing today.
I cannot face it on my own. Give me Your grace
and send Your peace to comfort me in my confusion.
You have said that Your grace is sufficient
and that Your strength is made perfect in our weakness.
Father, I feel so weak today.
You know exactly what I need even before I ask.
My prayer is that You will give me a calm spirit
and a clear mind so that I can see which way to go.
Be my rock, Lord, and let me hold onto You.
Your Word is a lamp for my feet and a light to my path.
Guide me in Your truth.

A Prayer for Wisdom

Lord, I am struggling today with a decision I must make.
There are so many ways I could go.
Is there a best way, Lord? If so, will You show me?
You have said that You will make our paths straight
if we commit all our ways to You.
I am laying this decision at Your feet, Father.
Open my eyes to Your truth. Send Your Holy Spirit to guide me.
Help me to accept the decision I make
and to do everything in my strength to make it right.
If You close a door, I know You will open a window.
Your ways are higher than my ways.
Give me Your peace and clear vision to see the road ahead.
Thank You for being my strength.

A Prayer for the Needs of Others

Dear Father, someone I love is in need of Your touch today.
Please bring Your grace to my friends.
Help them to wait before You and to seek Your strength
instead of trying to do it by themselves.
You can provide for their needs because You are God.
If it is Your will, You can heal or You can change circumstances.
Show them that you are in control and give them Your peace.
Help them to have the courage to know what they can change
and the serenity to know what they can't.
Give them a deeper knowledge of who You are through this
struggle.
Strengthen their trust and help them to glorify You in all their
trials.

Suggested Readings and Resources

Aranza, Jacob and Josh McDowell. *Making a Love That Lasts: How to Find Love Without Settling for Sex.* Ann Arbor, Mich.: Servant Publications, 1996.

Arterburn, Stephen and Fred Stoeker. *Every Young Man's Battle: Strategies for Victory in the Real World of Sexual Temptation.* New York: Waterbrook Press, 2002.

The Bible Promise Book. Urichsville, Ohio: Barbour and Company, Inc., 1990.

Dobson, James Dr. *Life on the Edge: A Young Adult's Guide to a Meaningful Future.* Dallas: Word Publishing, 2000.

Doud, Guy. *Stuff You Gotta Know: Straight Talk on Real Life Issues.* St. Louis: Concordia Publishing House, 1993.

Dunn, Sean. *I Want the Cross: Living a Radical Faith.* Grand Rapids, Mich.: Fleming H. Revell Co., 2001.

Fuller, Cheri and Ron Luce. *When Teens Pray.* Sisters, Ore.: Multnomah, 2002.

Graham, Franklin. *Living Beyond the Limits: A Life in Sync with God*. Nashville, Tenn.: Thomas Nelson Publishers, 1998.

———. *Rebel with a Cause*. Nashville, Tenn.: Thomas Nelson Publishers, 1995.

Haas, David. *Prayers Before an Awesome God: The Psalms for Teenagers*. Winona, Minn.: St. Mary's Press, 1998.

Hanegraeff, Hank. *The Prayer of Jesus*. Nashville, Tenn.: W Publishing Group, 2001.

Hunt, Angela Elwell. *Keeping Your Life Together When Your Parents Pull Apart: A Teen's Guide to Surviving Divorce*. iUniverse, 2000.

Johnson, Kevin Walter. *Get God: Make Friends with the King of the Universe*. Minneapolis: Bethany House, 2000.

———. *Does Anybody Know What Planet My Parents Are From?* Minneapolis: Bethany House, 1996.

———. *Can I Be a Christian Without Being Weird?* Minneapolis: Bethany House, 1992.

Lucado, Max. *He Chose You* (adapted from *He Chose the Nails*). Nashville, Tenn.: Thomas Nelson Publishers, 2002.

Luce, Ron. *Extreme Promise Book*. Nashville, Tenn.: J. Countryman Press, 2000.

———. *The Mark of a World Changer*. Nashville, Tenn.: Thomas Nelson Publishers, 1996.

McDowell, Josh and Bob Hostetler. *13 Things You Gotta Know to Make It as a Christian.* Nashville, Tenn.: W Publishing Group, 1992.

Myers, Bill. *Just Believe It: Faith in the Real Stuff.* Eugene, Ore.: Harvest House, 2001.

Peterson, Lorraine. *How to Get a Life . . . No Strings Attached: The Power of Grace in a Teen's Life.* Minneapolis: Bethany House, 1997.

Shellenberger, Susie. *Help! My Friend's in Trouble! Supporting Your Friends Who Struggle with . . . Family Problems, Sexual Crises, Food Addictions, Self-Esteem, Depression, Grief and Loss.* Ann Arbor, Mich.: Servant Publications, 2000.

Speck, Greg. *Sex: It's Worth Waiting For.* Chicago: Moody Press, 1989.

Stroebel, Lee. *Case for Faith—Student Edition.* Grand Rapids, Mich.: Zondervan, 2002.

Thurman, Debbie. *Hold My Heart: A Teen's Journal for Healing and Personal Growth (for Girls).* Monroe, Va.: Cedar House Publishers, 2002.

———. *Sheer Faith: A Teen's Journey to Godly Growth (for Boys).* Monroe, Va.: Cedar House Publishers, 2003.

Trujillo, Michelle. *Teens Talkin' Faith.* Deerfield Beach, Fla.: Health Communications, Inc., 2002.

Waggoner, Brittany. *Prayers for When You're Mad, Sad or Just Totally Confused.* Ann Arbor, Mich.: Vine Books, 2002.

Wilkinson, Bruce. *Secrets of the Vine for Teens.* Sisters, Ore.: Multnomah, 2003.

Youngs, Bettie B. *Safeguarding Your Teenager from the Dragons of Life: A Guide to the Adolescent Years*. Deerfield Beach, Fla.: Health Communications, Inc., 1998.

———. *Taste-Berry Tales: Stories to Lift the Spirit, Fill the Heart and Feed the Soul*. Deerfield Beach, Fla.: Health Communications, Inc., 1999.

———. *A String of Pearls: Inspirational Stories Celebrating the Resiliency of the Human Spirit*. Holbrook, Mass.: Adams Media, 2000.

———. *Gifts of the Heart: Stories That Celebrate Life's Defining Moments*. Deerfield Beach, Fla.: Health Communications, Inc., 1999.

———. *Values from the Heartland*. Deerfield Beach, Fla.: Health Communications, Inc., 1998.

———. *Helping Your Child Succeed in School*. Deerfield Beach, Fla.: Health Communications, Inc., 1998.

Youngs, Bettie B. and Jennifer Leigh Youngs. *365 Days of Taste-Berry Inspiration for Teens*. Deerfield Beach, Fla.: Health Communications, Inc., 2003.

———. *A Taste-Berry Teen's Guide to Managing the Stress and Pressures of Life*. Deerfield Beach, Fla.: Health Communications, Inc., 2001.

———. *A Taste-Berry Teen's Guide to Setting & Achieving Goals*. Deerfield Beach, Fla.: Health Communications, Inc., 2002.

———. *A Teen's Guide to Living Drug-Free*. Deerfield Beach, Fla.: Health Communications, Inc., 2003.

———. *More Taste Berries for Teens: A Second Collection of Short Stories and Encouragement on Life, Love, Friendship and Tough Issues*. Deerfield Beach, Fla.: Health Communications, Inc., 2000.

————. *Taste Berries for Teens: Inspirational Short Stories and Encouragement on Life, Love, Friendship and Tough Issues.* Deerfield Beach, Fla.: Health Communications, Inc., 1999.

————. *Taste Berries for Teens #3: Inspirational Stories on Life, Love, Friends and the Face in the Mirror.* Deerfield Beach, Fla.: Health Communications, Inc., 2002.

————. *Taste Berries for Teens Journal: My Thoughts on Life, Love and Making a Difference.* Deerfield Beach, Fla.: Health Communications, Inc., 2000.

Youngs, Bettie B., Jennifer Leigh Youngs and Debbie Thurman. *12 Months of Faith: A Devotional Journal for Teens.* Deerfield Beach, Fla.: Faith Communications, 2003.

————. *A Teen's Guide to Christian Living: Practical Answers to Tough Questions About God and Faith.* Deerfield Beach, Fla.: Faith Communications, 2003.

Youngs, Jennifer Leigh. *Feeling Great, Looking Hot & Loving Yourself! Health, Fitness and Beauty for Teens.* Deerfield Beach, Fla.: Health Communications, Inc., 2000.

Support Resources

Focus Adolescent Services
An information and referral service for families of troubled teens, *not* a hotline.
877-FOCUS-AS (877-362-8727)
www.focusas.com

AIDS Hotline for Teens
800-234-8336

Alcohol and Drug Abuse

National Council on Alcoholism and Drug Dependence
Hope Line
twenty-four hours: 800-622-2255

Al-Anon and Alateen Family Headquarters
800-356-9996

National Association for Children of Alcoholics
301-468-0985
Teen Challenge International USA Headquarters
3728 W. Chestnut Expressway
Springfield, MO 65802
417-862-6969
www.teenchallengeusa.com

Child Abuse, Rape, Sexual Abuse

Childhelp USA
twenty-four hours: 800-4-A-CHILD

Rape Crisis Center
800-352-7273

Faithful and True Ministries
6542 Regency Lane
Eden Prairie, MN 55344
www.faithfulandtrueministries.com

Eating Disorders

American Anorexia and Bulimia Association
165 W. 46th Street, Suite 1108
New York, NY 10036
212-501-8351

National Eating Disorders Association
603 Stewart St., Suite 803
Seattle, WA 98101
206-382-3587
www.NationalEatingDisorders.org

Mental Health Issues

National Alliance for the Mentally Ill
Colonial Place Three
2107 Wilson Blvd.
Arlington, VA 22201
800-950-NAMI (6264)
www.nami.org
Check your phone book for local chapters.

Christian Mental Health Services, Inc.
2180 Pleasant Hill Road, A5-225
Duluth, GA 30096
770-300-9903
www.christianmh.org

Ministries, Family Counseling

Notfortheweak.com, an online teen community on issues teens face. The phrase "not for the weak" is to make the point that we're not afraid to tackle the toughest issues, both in our society and in our personal lives. At the end of the day, we want people to leave this site challenged to discover who they are and what their purpose is in this life, and to find freedom in Jesus Christ.

Focus on the Family
Colorado Springs, CO 80995
719-531-3400
www.family.org
Maintains a national referral network for counselors.

American Association of Christian Counselors
1639 Rustic Village Road
Forest, VA 24551
(434) 525-9470
www.aacc.net
Maintains a national referral network for counselors.

Pornography, Sexual Addictions

National Center for On-Line Internet Pornography
Usage and Addictions
eBehavior, LLC
P.O. Box 72
Bradford, PA 16701
877-CYBER-DR (292-3737)
www.netaddition.com

PureIntimacy.org
Developed by Focus on the Family

Porn-Free Ministries
www.porn-free.org

Turning Point
A Ministry of Teen Challenge
See contact information above.

Abstinence/Sexual Relationship Counseling

"What If . . ."
www.sexrespect.com / Promote Teen Abstinence
Promotes second-time virginity

Pregnancy Counseling

Birthright International
777 Coxwell Ave.
Toronto, Ontario M4C 3C6
Canada

Birthright USA
P.O. Box 98363
Atlanta, GA 30359
800-550-4900
Information about abstinence, safe sex, infant care and adoption services.

Runaway, Homeless Teens

National Runaway Hotline (twenty-four hours)
800-621-4000

Suicide

Suicide hotline: 800-SUICIDE

About the Author

Bettie B. Youngs, Ph.D., Ed.D., is a Pulitzer Prize–nominated author of thirty books translated into thirty-one languages. She is a former Teacher-of-the-Year, university professor and executive director of Instruction and Professional Development, Inc. A long-acknowledged expert on family and teen issues, Dr. Youngs has appeared frequently on *The Good Morning Show, NBC Nightly News,* CNN and *Oprah. USA Today, The Washington Post, Redbook, U.S. News & World Report, Working Woman, Family Circle, Parents Magazine, Woman's Day* and the National Association for Secondary School Principals (NASSP) have all recognized her work. Her acclaimed books include: *Taste Berries for Teens: Inspirational Short Stories and Encouragement on Life, Love, Friendship and Tough Issues; Safeguarding Your Teenager from the Dragons of Life; A Teen's Guide to Living Drug-Free; A Teen's Guide to Christian Living: Practical Answers to Tough Questions About God and Faith; 12 Months of Faith: A Devotional Journal for Teens;* the Pulitzer Prize–nominated *Gifts of the Heart: Stories That Celebrate Life's Defining Moments* and the award-winning *Values from the Heartland.* Dr. Youngs is the author of a number of videocassette programs and is the coauthor of the nationally acclaimed *Parents on Board,* a video-based training program to help schools and parents work together to increase student achievement.

To contact the author, write to:

Youngs, Youngs & Associates
3060 Racetrack View Drive
Del Mar, CA 92014

Web site: *www.tasteberriesforteens.com*

Inspiration and Guidance

Enjoy each day's inspiration as you take these taste-berry truth— and wisdom reminders to heart.

Code #0960 • Paperback • $12.95

Be smart! In *A Teen's Guide to Living Drug-Free*, you will find advice from experts, as well as stories and tips about living a drug- and alcohol-free life.

Code #0413 • Paperback • $12.95

For more great books by Bettie and Jennifer Youngs
Go to hcibooks.com

More Great Books From Bettie